Personal Injury Primer

-Vol. 1-

David W. Holub
Katelyn C.V. Holub

Personal Injury Primer

-Volume 1-

ISBN 13: 978-1-7324682-5-2

Printed in USA

Table of Contents

Introduction

Welcome to **Personal Injury Primer**, where we break down the law into simple terms, provide legal tips, and discuss topics related to personal injury law. What started out as a few podcast episodes a year ago, has morphed into a resource that colleagues, clients and, dare we say, even insurance agents can use.

Our primary goal is to educate the reader into learning more about personal injury law, how they can protect their rights and what to do if they find themselves the victim of negligence.

That negligence accounts for the majority of auto accidents, medical malpractice, product injury claims and wrong death cases we pursue.

An auto accident can change the course of a person's life in a split second. An injury can have far reaching impact on an entire family if a family member is unable to work, if hospital or home nursing care is required, or if the injured person's ability to contribute to the operation of the household is altered.

Negligence by a medical professional could be the result of an error in diagnosis, treatment or illness management. Negligence is based on a failure to follow accepted standards of practice. For example, a hospital may provide improper care in not properly assessing a fall risk resulting in a patient fall.

Products liability law involves the legal theories of strict liability, negligence, breach of warranty, fraud, misrepresentation, and violation of the deceptive trade practice laws. From a consumer standpoint, these cases generally concern whether appropriate warnings were given to users or consumers of products.

A wrongful death is the death of a person caused by the negligence, willful act, or wrongful act of another. Our firm has served a number of surviving family members in such circumstances and helped them deal with such events which are always traumatic and fraught with special challenges.

Join us as we share with you this insightful book that will answer a great many of your questions. And if you, or a loved one, live in Indiana, and were injured by the negligence of another pick up the phone and call us at (219)736-9700. Or visit us on our website at www.DavidHolubLaw.com

Our mission is to provide top quality legal representation, which includes an uncompromising pursuit of our client's legal interests, while being accessible and attentive to our clients during times of personal challenge.

David W. Holub

Katelyn C. V. Holub

Chapter 1

Motor Vehicles

Water Ponding on the Expressway

"I was on the expressway last night. It had rained hard, but had stopped raining for several minutes. All of a sudden, I hit this huge pond of water covering all lanes and then I hit the wall. Others wiped out too. What are my legal options?"

If you're involved in a crash that results because of water accumulating on an expressway, there are a number of legal issues which will need to be addressed.

First, if the government is involved, and it most always is when you are dealing with an expressway, the government cannot be sued except under certain special circumstances.

One of those circumstances is that you have to file a notice with the government that you intend to make a claim. This is called a tort claim notice.

It typically has to be filed within 180 days of an event.

For some government agencies it can be filed up to 270 days after the event.

However, due to the particularly time-sensitive nature of making a claim against the government, we recommend that you consult an attorney as soon as possible if you're involved in this kind of the crash.

Even if you give timely notice to the government, as required by the statute, the government can be immune from being held legally responsible for many roadway conditions.

When a hazard is created on a roadway because of an inclement weather event, such as a snowstorm or a rainstorm, the government generally can't be held responsible for your damages that are caused as result of that natural occurrence.

The real question is: are there ways around the barriers that the government puts up against suing it? Well, yes.

First, while the government can be declared immune from a crash directly caused by weather conditions, there are several exceptions to that rule. You will need an attorney to review the facts to see if any of those exceptions apply.

Second, if there's a contractor involved, the contractor may be subject to suit, even if the government is immune from suit.

For example, suppose a contractor or an engineer or a construction company improperly designed the highway, and built it so that it didn't drain properly. In such a case, that contractor or engineer might be liable.

Or, think about this situation. What if a contractor installed a special retention pond with a pump that was supposed to pump water away from the roadway, but the pump failed because it wasn't put in properly, or the switch that was supposed to trigger the pump failed because the sensor that was supposed to come on automatically didn't work. Or, what if the power went out to the pump and there was no emergency backup power available to the pump? All of these things can lead to potential liability for the contractors and engineers. It also could lead to government liability as well in some fact situations.

Rear-Ended, But Insurance Blames Me

"I was rear-ended and the other driver's insurance company is blaming me for the crash. How can they do that? What does that mean for me?"

Generally, when people think of a rear end collision, they assume that the driver who did the rear ending is 100% responsible for the collision. You may be surprised that the insurance company for the driver who did the rear-ending would argue that the person who got rear-ended is partly at fault, but think about it this way: if there is a way for the insurance company to not have to pay out as much, it will seize the opportunity.

One of the ways an insurance company can save money, is to show that the person who got rear-ended was partly responsible for the collision.

Is a person who got rear-ended ever partly to blame for the collision? Well, sometimes yes. It really depends on the specific facts of the case.

Think, for example, about someone who weaves from one lane to another in traffic. An insurance company might argue that a driver's fast weaving in and out of lanes caused another person to rear-end them because they didn't have enough time to stop when someone quickly switched to their lane and was too close in front of them.

If the person who is claiming to be injured is found partly at fault by a judge or jury, a key determination is quantifying that percentage of partial responsibility. In other words, was the injured party 30% at fault in causing the rear end collision? 50% at fault? 60% at fault? In Indiana, so long as the other driver is found to be 51% or more at fault for the collision, an injured person can recover for their losses and injuries.

Notes:

While an insurance company may be claiming you are to blame, that does not mean they will be able to convince a jury or judge of your fault. A good attorney will be able to discuss with you the strengths and weaknesses of your case, including any potential degree of fault.

Hit by Road Debris

"I was driving behind a semi-truck on the highway when a part fell off the truck and flew into my car, injuring me. What are my legal rights?"

Over the years, we have represented several people who were injured while they were in a vehicle traveling behind a tractor-trailer on a highway when a part, such as a drive shaft, flew off the semi-truck and struck our client's vehicle. When parts strike a vehicle after flying off a semi-truck, devastating injury and/or death can occur.

In these types of situations, the key legal issues often boil down to either negligent maintenance of the semi-truck or the manufacture of a defective part.

With regard to negligent maintenance situations, regulations at the state and federal level require that tractor-trailers undergo regular maintenance and safety checks before being driven on our highways. If not properly maintained, parts like drive shafts can come loose and ultimately fall off tractor trailers—becoming a dangerous flying projectile for anything in its path. Not only does the flying projectile part from the truck pose a danger to others on the road, but also the truck itself, as it can jack-knife or otherwise lose control because of it.

Our attorneys are familiar with the detailed maintenance standards that apply to tractor-trailers and the trucking industry. Our knowledge enables us to lead an effective investigation into what went wrong in a given injury incident, which, in turn, equips us to craft more compelling arguments to hold those responsible for the harm to account for the damages done.

Another issue that sometimes comes up in these types of cases is whether the manufacturer of a vehicular part failed to safely design or make the part. We've all heard of recalls for various auto parts over the years. For example, there have been big airbag and tire recalls in the recent past. Well, sometimes semi-truck parts fail as a result of improper design or manufacture, regardless of how well the truck was maintained.

Notes:

The bottom line is that these types of cases require thoughtful legal analysis and investigation on the part of a lawyer in order to determine who to hold accountable for injuries, such as the truck driver, trucking company, and/or manufacturer of a vehicular part.

Making a Hit and Run Claim

"I was sitting in my parked vehicle in a parallel parking spot along a street and some other vehicle hit me and sped off. I have no idea who hit me, but I'm injured and my car is damaged. What can I do?"

In a typical hit and run collision, you don't know who the person is who hit your vehicle. They fled the scene before any identification could be made. In some situations, you might be able to eventually track down the person who hit you if you get their license plate information, in which case you would proceed to make a claim against that driver (and their insurance).

But what if you don't know the identity of who hit you?

In Indiana, the type of insurance coverage that often covers hit and run collisions by unknown drivers is called uninsured motorist coverage, and it is usually a part of your own automobile insurance policy.

These types of cases involve bringing a claim against your own insurance company, rather than the other driver's insurance company, since the other driver fled the scene and is unknown.

Not all uninsured motorist coverage provides for hit and run situations. Each individual policy has different language. Those that do cover hit and run collisions usually require that there be **physical contact** between your vehicle and the one that fled the scene.

So why do most policies require physical contact, you might ask? Physical contact is often a requirement in order to lower the instances of insurance fraud, in which people are just making up a story that they were hit. The insurance company wants to make sure that there has been a genuine HIT and then a run.

Now, if the "hit" or physical contact wasn't *directly* from the other vehicle, but the other vehicle kicked up some debris (like a rock) that hit and cracked your windshield, then that can be sufficient physical contact to make a claim, depending on your policy language.

If there's no physical contact between your vehicles, then the issue of whether there's coverage for the incident gets a little trickier and the policy language has to be examined carefully to see if a claim can still be brought.

For example, if another driver cuts you off and forces you off the road, then that would be an accident caused by an unknown driver, but it doesn't involve any physical contact. Even when there's been no physical contact, some policies still allow a claim to be made. Again—you may notice a theme here—it all depends on the specific language of your policy.

In situations like a hit and run claim, where you are potentially bringing a claim against your own insurance company, it is important to get an attorney. Because each policy has unique language and coverage options, don't just assume that you're out of luck because you don't know who hit your vehicle. Most attorneys don't charge you anything for an initial consultation, and you should show the attorney your insurance policy so that they can determine what coverage you have and can advise you further.

Also, in these hit and run collision cases it is crucial to consult with an attorney promptly after the collision because time can be of the essence in making a claim. Oftentimes, insurance policies are written with very short deadlines for hit and run claims—some requiring you give them notice within 90 days of the incident.

Notes:

When you are the victim of a hit and run driver the prospects of obtaining compensation for injuries sustained in the crash depend in large part upon whether you have "uninsured motorist" coverage and the language that describes this coverage in your insurance policy.

Hit by a Self-Driving Vehicle

"Who is legally responsible when a self-driving car causes a crash?"

Self-driving cars, robotic cars, or what they call autonomous driving vehicles, are supposed to be very common by 2025. In fact, many manufacturers expect that 5G wireless networks will make self-driving cars the primary means of transportation.

For now, we are just seeing occasional headlines about self-driving cars. Soon, we'll either have a self-driving vehicle or know of people who have one, but will a self-driving car be able to avoid collisions without human intervention and do so safely and securely without risking injury to passengers?

Do you really want a robot driving you around in a four-wheeled vehicle at highway speeds on a scenic, cliff-side highway?

Do you want to risk injury to your family because of a crash caused by some algorithm or formula that does not recognize correctly the edge of a cliff? Or, misreads a red traffic signal as green? Or rear-ends you because you forgot to turn on your headlights (and tail-lights) when you left the grocery store and it could not discern your car on the highway?

When a crash happens, how do you hold a machine responsible for injuring a person?

Our educated guess, and that is all it is, is that the law will hold the owners of the vehicle legally responsible for mistakes the robotic vehicle made in driving. And, the law will hold manufacturers responsible for manufacturing defects that contributed to cause the crash.

Right now, when a car component such as an airbag malfunctions, the car maker and the component supplier (for example, the supplier Takata in the case of the Takata airbag recall) can be held legally responsible. So, would you buy a self-driving car system made by Takata?

Uninsured and Underinsured Motorist Coverage

"What is uninsured and underinsured motor vehicle insurance and why should I care about getting it?"

When you buy the minimum liability insurance policy required by law to operate a vehicle on Indiana highways, that policy covers the other party if you end up in an crash.

If the other party has no insurance, then you are left out to dry, unless you purchase uninsured and underinsured motorist coverage, which will cover your losses if the other driver is driving without insurance.

Of course, nobody should drive without insurance. But, just like nobody should drive drunk, driving without insurance is something that happens all the time.

Let's imagine the worst. It's midnight and you're worried. Your husband should have been home two hours ago. You've tried to call him, but no answer. Then your phone rings. It's your husband calling. But the voice on the other end is not your husband's voice. You hear, "Ma'am, your husband has been in a serious car accident, could you come to the hospital please?"

Your emotions are all over the place. You have a thousand questions. You make it to the hospital. The receptionist directs you to the third floor. You find a police officer waiting for you.

The officer explains that a drunk driver hit your husband's car. Both cars were destroyed in the collision, and your husband is in critical condition. He needs surgery. He has multiple fractures, a collapsed lung, head trauma, plus scores of lacerations.

Your husband's life will be different, at least for the foreseeable future. He will require physical therapy, rest, pain management and weekly doctor's checkups. Your daily routine will need to be adapted to account for your husband's various appointments.

Unfortunately, lives are upended all too often by drunk drivers.

Drunk driving cases pose difficult legal challenges sometimes because while fault is frequently clear, a person who is irresponsible and drives drunk, is also statistically likely to be financially irresponsible and have no insurance on their vehicle.

For this reason, in Indiana, it is very important to maintain uninsured and underinsured motorist insurance coverage. This coverage protects the victim when the driver who has hit them has insufficient or no insurance.

In cases where a drunk driver has no insurance, or inadequate insurance, the next step is to investigate who served the alcohol. Was the drunk driver at a wedding, party, bar, or tavern? Was the person served alcohol while being observed to be intoxicated? Cases against bars and taverns are called dram shop cases. And dram shop cases, as well as any other case where proof of serving alcohol is important, must be investigated quickly, before memories fade and proof disappears.

So, in the case above, where the drunk driver collided and caused an accident, the victim would come to us seeking legal representation. We would then start an investigation. We would ask a lot of questions. We would request medical records, a police report, and any information that would help support our client's claim. However, with drunk driving cases there is often nobody with insurance or money that can be held responsible for the damage that was done.

Buying uninsured and underinsured motorist coverage protects you and everyone in your vehicle if there is a crash and the other driver has no insurance or inadequate insurance.

Notes:

We recommend buying the highest amount of uninsured and underinsured motorist coverage as you can afford. It is coverage that protects you and your family. It is heartbreaking when there is no coverage available to pay medical bills and other expenses after a crash due to lack of insurance coverage.

Holub

Chapter 2

Distracted Driving

Driving with Detectable THC Levels

"I was thinking about getting a commercial driver's license to drive a semi-truck, but they have drug screening requirements. How does that work now that marijuana is legal?"

Suppose a driver consumes marijuana in a state where it has been legalized, then drives into a state like Indiana where it is not legal. The driver gets into a crash and then THC is discovered in the driver's blood. What next?

First, even in the state where possessing marijuana is legal, it is not legal to drive under the influence of the drug. When a state lets a person get high, it does not let that person drive while high.

Second, people don't realize that marijuana can be traced in a person's blood system by a drug screen for 30 days or more after use. This means that while a person may have used the drug a week ago and not currently be under the influence of the drug, he or she could still test positive for the drug. This can be problematic in more than one way.

For example, the trucking industry has been having some difficulty recently getting young truck drivers who can qualify for over-the-road driver positions because many job applicants are not passing the restrictive drug screen for marijuana.

Of course, large commercial vehicles can be much more dangerous to operate compared to passenger cars. Drug screens are required not just to make sure a trucker is not driving under the influence, but to make sure they are not in the habit of using drugs in general.

Screening for all types of controlled substances is critical in the case of commercial vehicle operators.

Keep in mind, also, that although some states have identified marijuana as a drug that they will consider legal, it is not legal under federal law. Motor carrier regulations require drug screens. A person who uses marijuana products who thinks that they're going to pass a drug screen is sadly mistaken.

We've had many situations where drivers involved in car crashes that we are investigating have tested positive for THC, which is the dangerous ingredient in marijuana that is picked up in drug screenings.

If a person is going to smoke marijuana, or consume it in any manner, and then drive, they better think again. It can impair judgment and reaction time, just like alcohol. It is not legal anywhere to drive while impaired by alcohol or any other mind-altering drug.

Hands-Free Phones Distract

"I was in a crash and the other driver seemed distracted at the time. It looked like he was talking to someone when he hit me. When I asked him, he said he was using a hands-free cellphone and that he was driving safely. How can that be if he was distracted when he hit me?"

While we all have been told that it is not safe for drivers to use a *hand-held* cellphone while they are behind the wheel, does that mean *hands-free* cellphone driving is safe? Not surprisingly, many drivers have turned to using hands-free cellphones. The companies that sell hands-free devices claim they are a safe alternative to hand-held cellphones, but is that true?

The AAA group published a study not long ago that strongly suggests that using a hands-free cellphone while driving causes a significant amount of cognitive distraction and may lead to a car accident. During the study, researchers measured participant heart rate, eye movement, and brain activity while operating a car that had monitoring equipment on it. The participants were given various tasks to complete to test how their concentration was impacted while they performed the task and operated a motor vehicle. The results showed that drivers who used a hands-free cellphone were only slightly less distracted than when they used a hand-held cellphone.

It seems that the brain cannot fully focus on two complex tasks simultaneously. The brain allocates competing attention to both tasks on an alternating basis.

In other words, for a discrete amount of time the brain focuses on driving, then for the next few seconds it focuses on talking, listening, and formulating language responses, then switches focus back to driving. This frequent change in focus leaves cognitive gaps where drivers are not concentrating on the road. Thus, the risk of a serious accident is not greatly different between hands-free and hand-held calling. Both contribute to the problem of distracted driving and can result in more vehicle collisions.

Notes:

When it comes to talking on a phone while driving, both hand-held and hands-free phones can distract drivers and cause crashes.

Distracted by Social Media

"With all the public service announcements about the dangers of distracted driving, why does it seem that more and more people are driving distracted?"

Distracted driving accounts for a large percentage of the motor vehicle injury cases we help people with and it is tragic.

Distracted driving has been around since the dawn of the automobile, but over the last few years it's been on the rise. The culprit? The proliferation of social media- accessible mobile devices.

Recently a Facebook friend posted:

> I nearly got killed today while driving. A teenager on her phone almost broadsided me. If I had not veered hard and drove off the road, her SUV would have hit the driver side of my car head on. I was so shook up that I had to get out of my vehicle and calm down. When are people going to understand driving & talking on the phone impairs you like drugs and alcohol. Your focus goes to the phone and not your driving. The teenager never even stopped.

Sadly, more and more people are witnessing first-hand the epidemic that cell phone usage is adding to driver's distractions while behind the wheel. This is precisely why manufacturers of mobile devices are taking somewhat of a proactive stance by adding apps and sensors that detect when a vehicle is moving so that notifications of incoming calls, texts, and social media updates are temporarily shut off to those devices. However, it's the user's responsibility for using these apps and sensors.

Luckily for my Facebook friend, she still has fantastic reflexes and was able to swerve away from a head-on collision. But, what if she wasn't able to safely swerve out of danger? What if there was no shoulder on which to pull over? What if she had collided with the oncoming vehicle?

Over the years, I've shared many articles about distracted driving, and yet it seems more and more people (not just teenagers) are entering the roadways while engaging in some sort of activity on their smartphone.

Social media has given us the ability to connect rapidly with our fans, friends, and followers and when we hear a ding we have to immediately check to see who is sending us what. Unfortunately, we've become conditioned like Pavlov's dogs to check our devices constantly.

In 2015, a study revealed that the average cell phone user checks his or her phone 45 times per day. But by 2017, that statistic jumped to 85 times a day. Even more astonishing, Millennials (those between 24-39 years old) will check their devices up to 150 times per day.

Distracted driving is by all means negligent driving. Any time you take your eyes off the road to glance down at your phone you are putting yourself, your passengers, and the traffic around you in danger. Depending on how fast you're traveling, a split-second glance at your phone could be all it takes to veer into another lane and cause a crash.

Driver Assistance Systems Increase Distracted Driving

"With all the years of experience your office has in helping people who have been in car crashes, are you getting the sense that the number of crashes on the highway is going down, given all the safety equipment on cars these days?"

Safety equipment like airbags and anti-lock brakes do not reduce the number of crashes, but most likely reduce the severity of injuries suffered in crashes. In contrast, "driver assistance" safety systems are not likely making us safer. Many vehicles today commonly come with what are called "driver assistance" systems, which are designed to prevent crashes.

Fewer crashes is good, right? However, a recent report from AAA suggests that people's reliance on driver assistance systems may be increasing rates of distracted driving.

What if protective technology is really just lulling drivers into a false sense of security? Why look at the road if the car will protect you? Full driving automation will soon remove occupant control. When that happens, will we continue to call an occupant of a self-driving car a driver?

In the meantime, before complete automation, there's still a big safety burden on the driver to control the vehicle and remain situationally aware. That burden on the driver to drive safely is present even though there is some automation equipment on the vehicle that may help prevent collisions.

Data from recent studies indicates that the use of advanced driver assistance systems is associated with a 50% increase in the odds of engaging in a secondary task and an 80% increase in the odds of engaging in visual or manual secondary tasks, compared to the same drivers driving without an automated system.

What does that mean?

Well, if you think your car is going to watch for children running into the street to chase a ball and that the brakes will come on automatically, then you as the operator might think that it is safe to look down and read through the weather headlines displaying on the vehicle's entertainment console instead of watching the road.

For now, drivers actually operate vehicles more safely when the driver assistance systems are turned off. Again, this makes sense. If you have cruise control on and you know the car will automatically slow you down if you get too close to the semi ahead of you, then your brain disengages a little from your driving, which reduces safety overall.

The same holds true for driver assistance systems that are designed to alert drowsy drivers. If you have a drowsy alert system, you might think you are safe and keep driving, instead of pulling off the highway like you did years ago when you sensed yourself getting tired.

Here is another example. Have you ever had the need to drive a car using a spare tire or run-flat tire? If you know your tire might burst if you are going faster than is safe for the tire, then most people will drive extra-cautiously. Conversely, if you just replaced a bad set of tires or got new brakes, you likely will feel it is okay to drive faster and push the limits of your vehicle.

The take-away is that safety systems can erode our attention. That's dangerous. Smart car; not so smart human.

Notes:

It is only going to get worse. The smarter your car, the less the human operating it will be paying attention. It is human nature.

Chapter 3

Premises Liability

Injured by a Dog

"I was delivering a package for Amazon when this huge dog came out of nowhere and tore into me. My medical bills are mounting. Can I sue?"

Dog attacks on delivery people are becoming more and more common.

It used to be that only postal workers were attacked. Now with all the different delivery companies bringing packages to our homes, such as Amazon delivery, grocery delivery services, and FedEx and UPS, attacks on delivery people by dogs are becoming more common.

In dog bite situations, one of the key issues that we look at is whether there is insurance that covers the homeowner who owns the dog who bit someone. Unfortunately, many times there is no insurance that covers a dog. Either there's no homeowner's insurance policy, or there is an exclusion on the homeowner's policy that excludes coverage for dogs that bite. Sometimes we find an insurance policy provides coverage for dogs in general, but excludes certain dog breeds that may have a propensity towards being aggressive.

So why are we investigating the insurance situation and reviewing any relevant policies? It is important to determine if there is insurance because in many cases the people who own dogs that do not have insurance are in bankruptcy, on the verge of filing for bankruptcy protection, or otherwise have no way of paying for the damages their dog caused.

Besides analyzing potential insurance coverage, we also have to analyze the history of the dog.

Has the dog bitten other people before? If so, in what other situations has this dog shown aggression and attacked someone?

Did the owner have reason to know that they were keeping a dangerous dog on the property? There is an old line of court cases that developed a rule called the "one bite" rule, meaning unless the dog had bitten someone in the past, it was presumed not to be a biter. But, if the animal had bitten in the past, the owner was presumed to know the dog posed a danger.

If we can establish facts that show that the dog was known to be dangerous, then we investigate further to find out what steps, if any, the dog owner took to restrain their dog. For example, did they keep it locked up or leashed?

Did the dog break free from an enclosure?

Was the dog chained or leashed, but broke free just before the attack?

Did the property owner post warning signs that delivery people could view to put them on notice that they might encounter a dangerous dog on the property?

These are just a few examples of the kind of investigative work that we do in analyzing dog bite situations in order to preserve and optimize the legal rights of dog bite victims.

Notes:

Investigating whether dog owners have either the insurance coverage or money to pay for the damages caused by their dog is crucial. Even if a case appears to be a slam-dunk, without the ability of the wrongdoer or wrongdoer's insurer to pay for the harm done, it's over before it's begun.

Escalator Injury

"Mom and I were shopping at the mall. We took the escalator and all of a sudden it sped up. I held on, but mom fell and broke her shoulder. What are our rights?"

Escalators, like stairways, ladders, and elevators, must be properly maintained. If an escalator suddenly accelerates while people are riding up or down on it, the unexpected motion can cause the people riding on the device to fall.

Though sometimes an escalator will malfunction even if it is properly maintained—for example, if a component breaks—we have found that the majority of equipment malfunctions occur when there has been a failure to follow the standards for proper maintenance of the escalator equipment.

Most of the time an escalator will be controlled by chains and sprockets, or a system of pulleys and belts. When parts get worn, they can fail. We, as attorneys, are quite familiar with the maintenance standards that apply to these pieces of equipment and our knowledge of that helps fuel our investigation of each escalator injury incident.

Unfortunately, with many large retail stores experiencing financial stress, the temptation to cut corners in maintaining equipment, such as escalators or elevators, can be great.

If an escalator fails due to poor maintenance, a lawsuit against the owner of the device, and any repair contractors, is likely the best option. But if a part, such as a chain, broke despite the escalator being properly checked and maintained, then the escalator *manufacturer* may be subject to suit.

In any event, after investigating what exactly went wrong to cause a particular escalator injury, we can begin the legal analysis regarding which entity can be held responsible for an injury —such as the owner and/or manufacturer.

Injured at a Vacation Rental House

"We are thinking of renting a house through one of those B and B services, and we are wondering what legal standards apply if someone gets hurt on the property?"

When you stay overnight at a hotel you might be exposed to unsafe parking lots, unmarked curbs, potholes and even poorly lit hallways inside the buildings. People even are at risk for getting bitten by bedbugs, injured by exercise equipment, or sickened from swimming in non-chlorinated pool water.

Although that all sounds bad and you ought to be careful when you book a room at a hotel or motel, what are the risks of choosing a house rental service like Airbnb, VRBO (Vacation Rental By Owner), FlipKey, or many of the others advertised on the internet?

Interest in vacation house rental services has grown in the last several years. People enjoy having the comforts of a home setting without the negative aspects of staying at a hotel. However, keep in mind that by choosing a house rental, you are trading security for comfort, and that may come at a price.

You see, the host of the house rental typically doesn't have a full-time or even a part-time maintenance person to go around fixing things. Nor does the host usually have a housekeeping staff to make sure your bed is made and bathrooms are clean during your stay. Likewise, house sharing services don't typically have lifeguards for their pools or nighttime security staff. They might not undergo regular electrical and fire safety inspections either.

And unlike guests at hotels and motels, users of house sharing services usually give up their right to sue if injured on the rented properties as part of agreeing to the "Terms of Service" on the house sharing services website.

So, if you're a guest staying at a house sharing service and you are injured, could you be prohibited from suing those companies for your injuries? Possibly yes. You may have signed away your right to sue.

You might have assumed that the owner of the house would be protected by their homeowner's insurance and that any injury that occurs on the property would be covered, but did you know that most homeowner's insurance policies exclude coverage for "business activities" operated out of a home?

Renting your home for a profit is considered a business activity. Yes, insurance companies have a right to know when insuring a property whether you are bringing people (maybe a lot of people) onto the property to make money. It can impact premium rates. It can impact coverage.

That said, Airbnb announced recently that as part of using their service they would provide hosts with up to $1 million in liability protection if they get sued by a guest. But is $1 million enough? And what about the other house rental services?

Airbnb seems to be the only service offering such coverage, but whichever service you use, it's always a good idea to confirm that they are covered by insurance.

Injured at a Hotel or Motel

"What are my legal rights if I am injured while a guest at a hotel or motel?"

Many types of injuries can occur in overnight lodging situations, from bed-and-breakfast accommodations to inns and resorts. For example, a robbery or mugging can occur while you are on the premises of a hotel or motel.

Dangerous parking lot conditions, such as unmarked curbing or potholes, can cause people to fall while walking from their vehicle to their room. In addition, people staying at hotels can get hurt while going up and down staircases that have been poorly maintained, or by venturing into a washroom that has just been mopped where an employee forgot to place a wet floor warning sign.

On top of that, all too frequently guests encounter hazards inside their hotel rooms, such as bedbugs, slippery shower surfaces, or cabinets that can be tipped or pulled over by a child.

Sometimes exercise equipment is defective, or a swimming pool has been opened to use without first being properly chlorinated or disinfected. These types of hazards can result in injury, and some of these injuries can be serious.

We recently helped a fellow who responded to a knock on his motel room door only to be robbed and shot when he opened the door. Unfortunately, out-of-town travelers are considered excellent prey for robbers because they tend not to want to return to testify in court if the criminal is caught and arrested. In this particular situation, the motel had a history of frequent robberies and was near an expressway where robbers would make a fast getaway. However, the motel did not warn guests of this danger and was subject to legal liability.

Another incident that we helped with not long ago involved a hotel guest who happened to be a volunteer fireman from another state. When a fire broke out in the hotel, he helped people out of the hotel by knocking on doors. When he came down the stairs to exit the building, he slipped and seriously hurt his back when he stepped on a mat that had hastily been put down on a freshly mopped and wet floor, which created a serious slipping hazard.

Moreover, not long ago, we had an inquiry from an individual who was bitten by bedbugs and suffered a severe allergic reaction that was life-threatening. Surprisingly, this insect bite incident occurred at a very high priced hotel that had simply failed to take care of the insect dangers, and failed to follow proper cleaning and hygiene requirements.

In still another case, we represented a handicapped individual who was provided a special handicap room with a shower chair that collapsed when he transferred to it, which led to serious injury.

Indiana law holds property owners, including hotel and motel owners, liable for physical harm to their guests because of a condition on their property.

Specifically, the law holds property owners liable for physical harm caused to their guests by a condition of property, if, but only if, three legal criteria are met:

1. The property owner knows about the condition or by the exercise of reasonable care should discover the condition, and should realize that the condition involves an unreasonable risk of harm to guests;

2. The property owner should expect that guests will not discover or realize the danger, or will fail to protect themselves against it; and

3. The property owner fails to exercise reasonable care to protect guests against the danger.

Owners or occupiers of property, including hotels, owe a duty to use ordinary care to maintain their property in a reasonably safe condition for the use of those who come upon it as guests. The owners or occupiers have a duty to warn guests of any latent dangers on their property or dangers that are not readily apparent to guests. In addition, the landowner's duty includes a duty to inspect the premises, ascertain possible dangerous conditions, and warn guests of those conditions. This duty is active and continuous.

Notes:

Injuries while staying at hotels and motels come in all types. Speaking with an attorney about your specific injury experience is important in order to determine whether there are grounds for holding the hotel or property owner liable.

Falling On Ice

"Last February, I was walking with my wife into a big box store when I hit some ice and came down, destroying my knee. What are my chances at trial?"

We live in a geographic location where snow and ice accumulation is a routine occurrence. Countless times when we have sued in such cases, the defense team shouts out "the condition was open and obvious and we have no duty to protect against such conditions."

You might be wondering if that is a legitimate defense. It can be, depending on the conditions and the situation. But, there are some countervailing points of law on the side of the person who falls on ice in such situations.

What if the property owner puts out salt and cleared off snow on all walkways, but missed the spot right where the person loses their footing and falls? In such a case, a pedestrian would reasonably conclude that the walkways are clear and safe, which makes the hidden danger of the missed spot extremely dangerous.

On the other hand, the defense team will point out that the property owner does not have to be perfect, but just has to use reasonable care in clearing and salting the walkways. That is true too. Both parties have to use reasonable care.

See how trials can be anything but simple?

Suppose an injury occurs on a sidewalk leading to store entrance where there is a downspout. Let's imagine that there was no snow on the day of the fall and water from the downspout formed a layer of ice on the sidewalk. Perhaps the property owner knew this was likely to happen, and did routinely happen in that area all winter.

Suppose the store employee witnesses admit that they knew ice often formed in this area of the sidewalk and that they were supposed to inspect it every couple of hours or put out a sign warning people away from the danger.

Add some more facts. What if video surveillance from the day of the fall shows dozens of other customers seeing the ice and walking around it, and the fall victim looking over at a car entering the parking lot and missing seeing the ice?

When you look closely at the video surveillance and add that to the special knowledge the business has or should have about the icy area, isn't it reasonable for a jury watching those video clips to conclude that it was just a matter of time before someone unsuspecting was going to get injured?

Notes:

The outcome at trial for a fall on ice injury is often tricky and depends a lot on the specific facts surrounding a fall.

Tip-Over Injuries

"I saw on the news that a museum display toppled over and injured a child who touched the display. Who is legally responsible when such things happen?"

Every once in a while, we hear about museum displays tipping over onto visitors. For example, a few years ago in Overland Park, Kansas, a five year old boy was at the museum with his mom when an exhibit piece toppled onto him after he touched it.

The video released by the museum on social media made the mom out to be a bad parent for not paying attention to what her child was doing. The museum's insurance company blamed the mom for not keeping the boy in check and insisted the family pay $132,000 for the replacement cost of the broken sculpture. Now, was the family at fault? Some might think so. And, the video does show the sculpture being knocked over by the boy as he grabbed onto it.

But, there were a few things left out of the viral video. First, there was a bridal shower and a birthday party going on in the museum. Second, the sculpture that toppled over and broke was not in any way secured in place, nor was protective glass placed around it for safety or security. Third, you would think that being a museum they would have at least put up "Do Not Touch" signs so parents could warn their kids not to poke and prod exhibits.

Now, in the normal course of breakage within a museum or commercial enterprise, typically insurance is called upon to cover injuries or damages. So, why make an individual pay? In this case, the museum's insurance company didn't feel it was justified that they cover their client's damages when it was, in fact, a curious child that broke the piece while the mother was distracted.

If the child had been seriously injured by the display tip-over because the museum didn't take safety precautions, then the $132,000 would no longer be an issue and most likely the museum and their insurance carrier would be on the hook for thousands if not millions in a personal injury trial case.

This matter is similar to a case we had in which a television tipped over onto a child, killing the child.

A television weighing 92 pounds fell from a dresser and resulted in a fatal head injury to an infant who was playing in front of the television on a play blanket spread on the floor. Analysis of the stability of the television established that as little as 10 pounds of force applied at the top of the television, where the channel and volume controls are located, would cause the television to tip-over. The subject television, like many of its counterparts, did not contain any product warnings about the tip-over hazard it posed.

Although the museum art piece that tipped over was not a television, in both cases the sculpture and television were placed on top of other items (a pedestal and a dresser, respectively) that created potential tip-over hazards.

Chapter 4

Medical Malpractice

Pharmacy Errors

"The pharmacy gave me the wrong medication. Instead of getting well, I got sicker and sicker. Can I hold the pharmacy responsible for what it did to me?"

Sometimes, a pharmacy dispenses the wrong medication, the wrong dose, or the wrong formulation of a medication that contains an ingredient to which the patient has a noted allergy.

Over the years, our firm has helped numerous people who were harmed by improper fulfillments of prescription medication.

In some instances, the totally wrong product is dispensed to a patient. At other times, a pharmacy dispenses a medication that has an ingredient which is a known allergen to a patient, and the patient's specific allergy has been noted by the pharmacist, yet the pharmacist ignores the noted allergy warning for the patient and dispenses a medication with that allergen in it anyway. Still other times, an incorrect dosage is dispensed to a patient.

In each of these cases, it is important to carefully analyze whether a mistake is due to the pharmacy, a poorly written prescription, or miscommunication between the physician and the pharmacist.

Since many communications between doctors and pharmacists are now electronic, medication dispensing mistakes are less frequently caused by poorly handwritten prescription notes.

One of the key things to keep in mind in these types of situations is that a pharmacist has an obligation under the law to follow a doctor's instructions in dispensing a prescription. If there is an allergy, or if there is a particular type of product that that the patient is allergic to, that restriction must be followed by the pharmacist, and if it isn't followed, and the wrong drug is dispensed, or the wrong dosage amount of the correct drug is dispensed, the pharmacy can be held legally responsible.

Notes:

It can be especially tricky for patients and their doctors when prescriptions are mislabeled by pharmacies. A label may indicate a drug is something that it is not, or may indicate the formulation is free of a particular allergen, when in fact that formulation actually includes the allergen. In our experience, people have suffered a long time from the harmful effects of taking the wrong medication because neither they nor their doctors think of the possibility that they may be taking a mislabeled drug, so it takes longer to diagnose and address the true problem.

Erb's Palsy Birth Injury

"My granddaughter was born after a very difficult and long labor, and during the delivery, the doctor yanked on her arm and now there is something wrong with her arm and she can't move it, can you help me?"

Sometimes during a delivery, the shoulder of a baby may become stretched or stuck behind the pelvic bone of the mother. It happens more frequently with large babies. This type of birth injury, called Erb's Palsy, happens in about one in every one thousand births in the United States.

The bundle of nerves that run from the spine through the shoulder and to the ends of the fingers is called the brachial plexus. These nerves send signals that allow movement of the arms and hands. When a baby's brachial plexus is stretched or torn the result is Erb's Palsy.

There are four types of Erb's Palsy:

- An avulsion injury is the most severe. This is when nerves are pulled out from the spinal cord. A complicated surgery will likely be needed to restore function.
- A rupture injury is when several nerves are torn. This injury will likely require surgery and therapy to restore function.
- A neuroma injury results when scar tissue blocks the nerves and may require surgery.
- A stretch injury is the least severe type, but it may take one to two years before complete function is restored.

If your child has Erb's Palsy, the treatment will depend on the severity of the problem. The recovery for most children, however, is three to nine months. In more severe cases, physical and even occupational therapy may be a necessary part of the treatment.

Since Erb's Palsy is a largely preventable birth injury, if your child suffers from Erb's Palsy, severe or mild, contact a lawyer.

Bringing a Medical Malpractice Lawsuit after the Two Year Time-Limit

"My doctor just did surgery and removed a tumor. When my surgeon looked at my old x-ray films from four years ago, he saw the same tumor and said that an earlier doctor completely missed it, can I sue?"

This woman luckily had a situation in which the tumor was finally found; however, she explained to us that she suffered tremendously during the four years preceding her surgery, during which time the tumor went undiagnosed. The suffering included massive headaches, dizziness, pain, and loss of balance.

She was very shocked when she discovered from her surgeon that a radiology film taken four years ago actually showed the tumor, but the radiologist completely missed it. The radiology report diagnosed no abnormalities. This woman had even gone to two other physicians, who in reliance on the radiology report that missed the tumor, made her go through other testing to investigate what was causing the pain since they too went by the radiology report that said she had no abnormalities.

Finally, a third doctor she went to ordered another radiology study and found a very large tumor.

Once this third doctor removed her tumor, he decided to look at the CT scan film taken four years ago and what this doctor found made him furious. The tumor was clearly visible in the old film. If the radiologist four years ago had paid attention, then he or she should have seen that the tumor was clearly visible and absolutely should have been noted.

So, does a radiologist making a mistake in reading a film constitute malpractice or substandard care? Most of the time, the answer is yes.

Though it is difficult to read radiology films such as those obtained through CT scans, x-rays, or MRI studies, a radiologist is paid to use his or her best skills to read the films to see if there's anything actually visible in the image.

In this instance, either the radiologist didn't actually look at the film, or just totally missed what was visible. Such lack of care usually amounts to substandard medical care and usually justifies a lawsuit.

But the real issue raised by this woman's situation was the fact that this medical error took place four years ago. Why is that important? Because, in Indiana, the statute of limitations for suing for medical malpractice is two years, except in cases involving children under age 6, who are given additional time to sue.

In this woman's situation, the time in which to file a lawsuit had technically expired by the time the tumor was found and removed.

However, there's a little-known exception to the two-year time-limit rule that courts have carved out. If the malpractice could not have been discovered within the two years, and was not discovered within the two years, a court will take a look at the issue and allow a person to proceed with a lawsuit if the court believes that it was not reasonable for the person to be expected to know that malpractice occurred.

For example, courts have created an exception to the two-year time limit rule when a person has a surgery and the doctor mistakenly leaves a sponge or clamp inside the patient, and nobody knows about it until years later.

But in this woman's case, where a radiology report is written showing that everything is normal on the film, when in fact looking at it again, it's very clear that the film was misread, it definitely justifies seeking out an attorney to go over all the facts and help decide if there is justification for filing a lawsuit even though the two year time frame in which to sue has expired.

Botched Surgery Cover-Up

"My doctor botched my surgery and then lied about what she did. Can I sue?"

What started out as a routine hernia operation became a litany of medical errors that almost put the patient at risk of losing his intestines.

The doctor who operated had performed hundreds of these hernia operations in the past and was known as the "go to" expert for this type of medical procedure. Unfortunately, what transpired during this event would not only haunt the patient for the rest of his lifetime, but would negate the expert status the doctor had worked so hard to achieve.

Somehow, during the operation, a surgical instrument was left inside the patient's body cavity underneath the implanted mesh fiber. The anesthesiologist discovered the patient was reacting differently to the anesthesia and was starting to wake up too early. Then the machines that monitor patient heart rhythms started to flash, beep, and alert the medical team that something was wrong with the patient.

An inventory was ordered for all instruments used in the procedure. All was accounted for, except one. More anesthesia was administered to keep the patient from gaining consciousness. The patient was x-rayed to assess whether an instrument was left inside his body.

As the patient was being x-rayed, his wife was in the health care facility's comfort room awaiting news. It was going on four and a half hours now and the surgery was only supposed to take two hours. She was worried. No one had come out to speak to her as to what was happening with her husband.

Around the five-hour mark, the patient was rushed into the emergency room and his incision reopened. The mesh that had been implanted to prevent the hernia from getting worse needed to be cut open so that the doctor could find the lost medical instrument. Unfortunately, in removing the instrument from the body cavity, part of the patient's intestine was cut and no one on the medical team noticed. Subsequently, a new mesh insert was implanted in the patient.

Six hours had now gone by and the patient's wife was getting antsy. She wondered what was going on with her husband and demanded answers. The doctor finally came out and flat-out lied to the worried wife, saying that her husband had reacted badly to the anesthesia and would be in recovery soon.

However, this was not to be the case.

The damaged intestine was now leaking into the patient's body cavity and he was beginning to run a fever. A nurse took the man's vitals and alerted the doctor yet again. Another x-ray was done, which alerted the doctor of the need to once again open up the patient.

So now the patient was opened up a third time. The mesh lining implanted to repair the hernia was removed and repair surgery for the intestinal tear was performed.

Finally, after almost ten hours, the patient was awake and recovering. The patient's wife was livid and wanted answers. Sadly, the doctor and her team decided not to be forthcoming and didn't want to share the reasons why the surgery took eight hours longer than it was scheduled.

In this particular medical scenario, the doctor seemed careless and not forthcoming. But, is it classified under the law as negligence?

Let's examine what negligence means in this case.

Negligence by a medical professional can be the result of an error in diagnosis, treatment, or illness management. Negligence is based on a failure to follow accepted standards of practice. For example, a hospital may provide improper care in not assessing a patient's fall risk and not taking proactive measures to prevent a fall. On the other hand, a health care provider may dispense a medication in error, fail to maintain sanitation, or provide sub-standard nursing care, any of which might give rise to a patient injury.

In considering the botched hernia surgery scenario described above, negligence did occur. The next question is whether the patient can sue.

The law involving medical malpractice is designed to protect patients' rights to compensation if they are injured as the result of negligence. But malpractice suits are rarely simple and they are costly to fight. Sometimes the time and money needed to pursue compensation for an injury that is minor or heals quickly should not be spent because the case expenses would likely exceed the amount of recoverable damages.

Physicians and hospitals rarely admit mistakes. Even in cases that seem to be clear-cut, you can expect a defendant to fight any claim of wrongdoing.

The field of medical malpractice does not only apply to doctors. It can also apply to nurses, dentists, osteopaths, physical therapy facilities, and others providing health care services.

Notes:

From botched surgeries to birth injuries, brain injuries to failures to diagnose, nursing home abuse injuries to medication dosage injuries, and everything in between, we have successfully handled medical malpractice claims covering a wide range of medical errors.

Injured by a Robotic Surgical Device

"I was injured during a robotic surgical procedure. Can I sue a robot?"

We have all watched science fiction movies featuring robots. Maybe the cute robots in Star Wars come to mind? Probably everyone would love to have an R2D2 robot to make life easier.

Today, robots are routinely used in surgeries, and it is not science fiction.

So, here is the question: What if a surgical robot injures you? Can you sue a robot?

Maybe a simpler question to answer first is whether you can sue a surgical glove or a scalpel.

Certainly you can sue the manufacturer or seller of a product if the products are defective and you have proof that the manufacturer failed to use care and made a defective product.

If a scalpel is supposed to be sterile, but instead is coated with a dangerous cleaning chemical, you could sue for the consequential harm. Likewise, you could sue for the injuries you sustained from surgery because a surgical glove had a hole in it and was not sterile.

In the same way that a surgical glove might have a hole in it, which causes a break in the sterile surgical environment and leads to an infection, a robotic device used in surgery very well could be defective and cause you harm. But, the maker of the robot may try to blame the doctor or surgeon who was using the device, arguing that the robot functioned perfectly and the doctor is the one who made the mistake. In such cases, the only option may be to sue both the doctor and the robot- maker and let them point fingers at each other in court.

A well-known robot brand that has had product recalls is Da Vinci. One recall was due to hot shears, or really curved scissors, leaking stray electricity that could cause thermal burns to nearby organs and other tissue. Robots run on electricity, and if the electricity isn't properly contained, it can burn things. A very dangerous potential defect!

If a person has a poor outcome after undergoing surgery with a robotic device, is it possible that the robot functioned correctly, and that the doctor simply misused the robot and caused an injury? Of course! The actual cause of an injury could be a problem with the robot or the person using the robot. Or, it could be a situation where both the robot and the human surgeon malfunctioned, or made mistakes, and *jointly* caused harm to the patient.

According to the Food and Drug Administration, the most commonly noted injuries occurring in robot-assisted surgeries are burns, intestinal tears, punctured blood vessels, ureter injuries, perforated bowels, and excessive bleeding.

If you suspect you have been injured by a robot or a human using a robot, we suggest that you call an attorney promptly.

Notes:

As technology advances within the fields of artificial intelligence and robotics, we can expect to see more robot-assisted surgeries being done and likely more robot-related injuries.

Holub

Chapter 5

Nursing Homes

Pressure Sores

"I hired a nursing home to take care of my dad, but he developed pressure sores while there and had to be taken to the hospital. The doctor told me that my dad was maybe abused. What are my legal options?"

Unfortunately, we hear situations more and more frequently about nursing home failures with regard to abuse and pressure sores. These situations are appalling.

When we look for places to take care of someone that we care about we all try to do whatever research we can to see that that place does a good job of taking care of those patients who have been entrusted to them.

Sadly, sometimes these nursing homes do not live up to our expectations and they fail to care for some of society's most vulnerable people.

The pressure to cut costs, the lack of solid employee training, along with the fact that the nursing home industry has a high employee turnover rate can result in substandard patient care that puts patients' health and lives at risk. But that in no way excuses the appalling facts of nursing home neglect and abuse.

Ever so quickly, a nursing home that a son or daughter legitimately thought would be a safe place for their ailing parent to receive care . . . a place that they should have been able to trust . . . can wind up being a place that fails to care for its patients like we would all expect and desire.

The condition that is known as a pressure sore or a bedsore is preventable. However, in order to prevent them, health care workers must utilize the right kind of risk assessment and practical techniques.

Just as employees at health care facilities assess and address whether a patient is a fall-risk to him or herself, the staff at health care facilities and nursing homes are also supposed to be assessing and addressing a patient's risk of developing pressure sores.

A health care facility, whether a hospital, nursing home, or other long-term care facility, should be giving a patient a pressure sore risk assessment within eight hours of admission. These assessments often are scored by what is known as a Braden Score, which looks at several criteria, including a patient's mobility. The lower the score, the more at risk the patient is for developing pressure sores.

Facilities should be reassessing a patient at regular and frequent intervals after admission, and whenever there is a significant change in the condition of the patient.

So, when we look at records to see if a facility has breached the standard of care, one of the things we look at is whether a proper assessment was regularly done.

If pressure sores were noted as a risk, we look to see what, if any, steps were taken to eliminate or lessen the risk.

The primary way pressure sores can be prevented is by moving a patient frequently so that the patient's skin is not made to suffer sustained pressure for too long of a time on any one area of the body.

For example, patients can be physically moved on a regular basis or placed on special mattresses that are designed to prevent pressure wounds.

Notes:

Things to look out for when concerned about possible nursing home abuse or neglect include: failing to regularly re-position the patient so as to eliminate excessive pressure, leaving a patient to lie in wet, soiled beds and/or wet diapers, and failing to provide proper nutrition and hydration to the patient.

Protecting Patients from Nursing Home Abuse

"My family member was hurt as a result of abuse or neglect at a nursing home. What are the family's legal rights against the nursing home?"

Nursing home injuries resulting from neglect or abuse are serious matters. But, not every nursing home injury justifies the filing of a medical malpractice lawsuit. Malpractice cases are expensive to pursue and require expert testimony to be successful. A good attorney carefully evaluates every situation, logically looking at the costs and benefits of pursuing a legal claim.

When an injury heals quickly, a malpractice case may not be practical.

But even in the absence of filing a lawsuit, there are remedies available to families who have had a loved one fall victim to abuse or neglect at an assisted living facility.

Here are a few of the steps a family should consider taking immediately to protect a patient's safety and well-being at a nursing home.

1. Contact the operators of the nursing home.

    If you suspect neglect or mistreatment, discuss the issue with the chief of staff at the facility or higher-level management at the facility. Your goal should be to resolve the problem and ensure better care for your loved one going forward.

2. Consider recording the conversations you have in-person about your issues.

> If you come to an agreeable understanding about the issue, ask the facility to put it in writing and ask them to sign it. Thereafter, you must continue to monitor the problem to be sure that the solution is implemented, and that the patient is safe and secure.

3. Contact state officials charged with supervising the facility.

> Consider contacting your state's adult protective services agency, and/or nursing home licensing board. Such agencies need to know of dangerous situations at a facility, and may be able to connect you with other resource agencies at the local and federal government levels.

4. Document with photos and videos signs of abuse or neglect.

> If you see bruising and/or swelling, or what might be called common warning signs of abuse or neglect, you need to take action to preserve evidence of what you observe. Factual proof that your elderly or vulnerable loved one may have been mistreated is important. Have the photos or video clips available when you discuss the matter with the operators of the facility and/or government regulatory agencies. Stay vigilant.

Notes:

If your loved one has suffered a serious injury while at a nursing home, or extended care facility, contact a qualified attorney as soon as possible for assistance in holding the operators of the facility accountable for any wrongful conduct.

Holub

Chapter 6

Products Liability

Airbag Injuries

"I was injured by the airbag during an auto accident. What legal rights do I have?"

We've had a number of cases over the years that deal with the failure of the airbag system on cars. The airbag systems in modern cars are complex. They are not supposed to activate at low speeds. At moderate speeds they are designed to expand with limited force. At high speed impacts they should expand with full force.

Of course, if a serious injury results due to the *failure* of an airbag to activate, that is a time to speak with an attorney. But what about injuries that occur when an airbag *does* inflate?

If a driver is small in stature, say under 5-feet tall, their risk of injury is great because the seat needs to be close to the steering wheel in order for their feet to reach the pedals, but that then puts their body closer to the steering wheel, which houses the airbag. The plastic cover that flies off of an airbag at the time of inflation, can do serious damage. In one case that we handled, the airbag housing fractured a young woman's elbow.

Sometimes these injuries can be prevented if a driver grips the steering wheel in a certain way. Most modern vehicle operating manuals recommend that a driver hold a steering wheel at or below the 9 o'clock and 3 o'clock levels in order to avoid injury. In the case we handled, the proper warning was not set forth in the owner's manual or posted in the vehicle.

Something also to note . . . if the airbags don't work in a car that is over 10 years old, you might not be able to sue. In Indiana there's a statute which lets car makers off the hook if a product is over 10 years old when it malfunctions. People routinely drive older cars, but safety-related equipment in older vehicles may not function as expected.

Notes:

A lot of automobile safety equipment, like seatbelts and airbags, has saved lives, but they can also malfunction and cause injury.

Product Labels

"I assembled a bunk bed according to the instructions provided, but the ladder came off and my kid fell and got hurt, what are my legal options?"

Sometimes we all laugh at instructions or warnings that state the obvious—for example, the instructions that say, "Do not hold the chain end of a chainsaw," or the label on a wheel barrow that says "not intended for use on the highway."

But imagine the chaos that would ensue in a world without any warnings or instructions on the products we purchase.

Consider, for example, the ramifications of not having instructions or warnings associated with the purchase of medications. What would happen if there were no instructions about the hazard of driving after you take a medication that makes you drowsy? Without such a warning, innocent people on the highways could be killed.

To protect consumers and the public, there are specific laws about the types of warnings and instructions required to be on a product label. For example, the Indiana Product Liability Act provides that a product is defective if the seller fails to:

> (1) properly package or label the product to give reasonable warnings of danger about the product; or
>
> (2) give reasonably complete instructions on proper use of the product;
>
> when the seller, by exercising reasonable diligence, could have made such warnings or instructions available to the user or consumer.

Ind. Code §34-20-4-2.

Evidence of the *absence* of a warning, in the face of evidence indicating the *need* for a warning, provides the legal basis upon which to hold a manufacturer or seller of a product liable for harm resulting from the *lack* of a warning or instruction.

So back to the issue about the bunk bed ladder coming loose. Suppose an investigation reveals that the assembly instructions included with the product are not clear. Further suppose that the manufacturer actually had holes drilled in the upper bunk rail and supplied bolts to fasten the ladder to the rail. But, except for the holes in the upper bunk rail, the upper rail looked *exactly* the same as the lower bunk rail. The beds were assembled in China, and nobody thought to supply any instructions in English. It's understandable that the consumer did not appreciate the difference between the upper and lower bunk rails, and the instructions were silent on the issue, and said nothing about fastening the ladder to anything with the supplied bolts. In such a situation, there would be a valid basis to bring a legal claim against the bunk bed manufacturer.

Notes:

There are additional legal grounds for establishing that a product label was defective or inadequate. For example, a needed warning could have been placed in a hard-to-see spot of a product label or placed on package inserts rather than the product itself. Seek out the advice of an attorney who will fully investigate all potential theories of your product liability claim.

Talcum Powder Linked to Ovarian Cancer

"My wife used talcum powder all her life, and died of ovarian cancer. Can I sue?"

You've probably heard about Johnson & Johnson's baby powder, also known as talcum powder, and an apparent link to ovarian cancer.

The story is that women who have routinely used talcum powder for a long time are at risk to develop terminal ovarian cancer. In one suit, $417 million in damages was awarded against Johnson & Johnson.

What is the legal issue involved in cases involving exposure to seemingly safe products, such as talcum powder?

Well, corporations, like Johnson & Johnson, have a duty to consumers to inform them about the risks associated with their products. Consumers rightly trust that a company will not market an unsafe product. But Johnson & Johnson broke this trust by allowing their talcum powder to be sold, despite being aware of its dangers.

In the talcum powder trials, lawyers have cited a 1982 study that demonstrated that women who used talcum powder on their genitals had a 92% increase in their risk of ovarian cancer. Moreover, a lead researcher of this study advised Johnson & Johnson to put a warning label on its product. Significantly, internal memos from Johnson & Johnson established that the company was aware of the carcinogenic danger associated with its product. An internal memo from the 1990's by a Johnson & Johnson medical consultant noted that denying the link between talcum powder and ovarian cancer is comparable to "denying the obvious in the face of all evidence to the contrary."

Fortunately, the jury that awarded $417 million held the company liable for failing to warn about the carcinogenic effect of its product. At last count, there were over 4,500 similar lawsuits pending against Johnson & Johnson. It is good to see a corporation held accountable for misleading consumers.

If you or loved one has used Johnson & Johnson baby powder and been diagnosed with ovarian cancer, you should consult an attorney about obtaining compensation for your suffering.

Notes:

When a company knows that its product poses dangerous risks, the law requires it to disclose those dangers to potential consumers.

Work Injuries Due to Defective Product

"My husband was injured when a chunk of wood flew out from a machine he using at work and was nearly driven clear through his stomach. We think the machine was defective. Can we sue the machine manufacturer and my husband's employer?"

Workers all across the country suffer serious injuries or are killed on the job as a result of defective industrial products each year. The type of industrial products involved in worker injuries includes manufacturing equipment, farming equipment and construction equipment.

Many times, when our legal team investigates a worker's compensation case, we discover that a defective industrial product is what led to the workplace injury. That can be a fortunate discovery because that piece of information allows the injury claim to go beyond the typical bounds of Indiana's workers' compensation laws, which are very minimal for injured employees.

What type of product defects are we talking about? You name it. Machinery can lack proper safety guards, safety instructions, or warnings. Sometimes we find that the fault lies with the employer for failing to instruct an employee on how to use a product properly.

Other times, we find that a machine was shipped to the employer with a safety guard, but the employer removed it. It's tough to hold a product-maker responsible for an employer removing a guard, unless the maker didn't post a warning instructing that safety guards are not to be removed. On the other hand, the maker can be held liable if it failed to install a safety interlock feature that would prevent the machine from starting if the safety guard was removed.

When a worker is seriously injured or killed on the job, it is important to look closely at the working environment. Was the machinery involved to blame? Was the worker simply not being careful? All such factors need to be looked at carefully.

The importance of examining third party claims when helping a worker pursue compensation benefits can't be overstated.

Third party claims permit an employee to be compensated for more types of injuries suffered than what is recoverable under Indiana's workers' compensation laws. For example, in a third party claim, an employee can recover for past and future pain and suffering, past and future mental anguish, loss of income, as well as loss of future income earning capacity. Additionally, third party claims allow spouses of injured employees to recover damages they suffered due to their injured spouse. These types of damages are not recoverable under workers' compensation laws, which set forth very limited benefits that an employer must legally pay as a consequence of an employee injury.

Although workers' compensation benefits are important and provide a way that employees can hold employers accountable for work-related injuries, employees who are injured by a defective product while at work have additional means for recovering for their injuries by being able to bring lawsuits against manufacturers, distributors, suppliers, and others who made the defective product.

Notes:

A good attorney will investigate all aspects of a workplace injury in order to see if a third party could be held liable for an employee's injuries, which would greatly increase the amount of recoverable damages beyond the limited amounts set forth under Indiana workers' compensation laws.

Holub

Chapter 7

Trains, Boats, Buses, and Bicycles

Injured on a Train or Bus

"I was hurt while riding on a commuter train when the door closed on me. Can I sue?"

The short answer is mostly yes, but sometimes no. We know this probably seems like an unclear answer, but here's why . . .

In Indiana, trains and buses are operated as quasi-governmental agencies. This is important since most people don't see buses and trains as government agencies. This is especially true if the name on the vehicle suggests that a private company is operating the commuter service. Even if the operator is technically a private company, in many cases a statute gives them protections as if they actually were the government.

This means that they qualify for governmental immunity. In general, in Indiana, like in many states, governmental agencies are immune from being sued unless you provide timely notice of the intent to sue.

Timely notice given to the government, in this case notice to a train or bus operator, allows for the opportunity to investigate the circumstances of the claim. Typically, notice needs to be given within 180 days of an incident, but there are exceptions.

Another component of governmental immunity is that many acts or omissions that typically would count as negligence, or a lack of reasonable care, simply do not qualify as wrongdoing when a government employee is involved.

For example, there is immunity for failure to make a safety inspection. For example, there's immunity if a train operator fails to inspect crossing gates when they should have been inspected.

Also, there is immunity for mistakes made in issuing a license. Suppose the government gives someone a license to practice medicine, when in fact the candidate does not qualify for a license. The government would be immune from liability over that.

So if you provide timely notice to the operator of the commuter train when you fall or are otherwise injured, you can sue for your injuries that were caused by the negligence of the employees and agents of the train operator. If you fail to provide timely notice, then you may be out of luck. Oh, and even if you make it past the notice hurdle, that doesn't mean your case against that governmental entity will be a breeze from that point forward. There are other landmines just waiting to blow up your case.

Notes:

Always consult with an attorney after you are injured on a train or bus to learn in detail about your legal rights and to make sure you don't lose what rights you have.

Hit by a Train

"My son's SUV was hit by a train. The gates didn't come down and there was no whistle. My granddaughter's injury is serious. I'm trying to help them get legal advice. Can they sue the train operator?"

When you hear about a car or SUV being struck by a train, you know the outcome is rarely going to be anything but tragic for the occupants of the motor vehicle struck by the train.

Yes, railroad operators can be sued and the sooner we can start investigating a case, the better things will go.

When we investigate railroad crashes, often we find that the crash could have been prevented, either by the installation of proper safety equipment, such as gates and flashers, or through proper maintenance of existing safety equipment, which we frequently find was neglected and failed to function as intended.

Also, when we are hired for a case involving a railroad we often find that there have been other reported crashes or close calls at the same intersection. Sometimes we discover there have been numerous complaints regarding the intersection—everything from complaints about gates and flashers not working for a period of time to complaints that the train routinely does not sound its horn as it approaches.

Under the law, a train has the right-of-way at railroad intersections *when it claims* the right-of-way by signaling its intent to cross the intersection by the sounding of its horn or whistle and/or by triggering crossing lights to flash and/or crossing gates to close.

Horns work well in most rural locations where there is very little traffic. However, in metropolitan areas, the most effective safety mechanism is gates that come down when the train approaches the intersection, or at the very least flashers that activate when the train approaches the intersection.

The activation of gates and flashers can be very complex.

First, the signaling equipment has to include sensors to reveal when a train approaches an intersection, crosses the intersection, and completes its crossing of the intersection.

All this information has to be known so that the crossing warnings activate when they are supposed to and then deactivate when the train is clear.

You do not want flashers to provide false warnings when there is no train because then drivers using the roadway will be conditioned to simply ignore the flashers.

It is important that the signaling equipment be routinely checked and maintained so that if sensors that note the presence of a train are malfunctioning, they can be quickly corrected, or if lightning has hit a steel rail and burned out a sensor, it can be promptly fixed.

Systems should be in place to alert the rail line headquarters of malfunctions. Failing to have such a warning system in place to alert a maintenance crew of a problem can amount to a breach of care. What is more, failing to promptly address a malfunction once the crew has been alerted to the issue can amount to a breach of care.

Over time, traffic patterns at particular railroad intersections change and require the installation of different signaling equipment. For example, in investigating railroad cases, we often find governmental studies of traffic patterns showing that traffic has increased on a rural road due to a new subdivision or real estate development. That increase in traffic affects railroad intersections in the area so as to trigger regulations that require flashers at the railroad crossing.

However, sometimes we discover that the railroad has delayed or refused to install flashers or gates at a particular crossing, despite knowledge of the new traffic situation.

As you can imagine, there are a variety of potential avenues for liability in railroad cases and not all cases involve issues with signaling equipment. Sometimes we find that the crew operating a train was simply negligent or was operating under the influence of drugs or alcohol and caused the crash.

Safe Boating

"What legal duties do boat operators have to prevent boating accidents and injuries?"

Each year, there are over 4,000 boating accidents, resulting in over 2,000 injuries and several hundred deaths, according to the United States Coast Guard. Our firm has represented people seriously injured in boating incidents, as well as family members of those who were killed.

In Indiana, boat operators are required to follow certain safety precautions. These safety rules include the duty of a boat operator to keep a proper lookout. It's imperative to ensure there aren't other boats, objects, or persons in and about the water that they might collide with.

Boat operators also have the legal responsibility to be aware of changing weather conditions and the dangers they may pose, such as increased waves, wave heights, and winds. For example, if you're operating a boat on Lake Michigan and a storm is forecast to hit the region soon, you are required to keep your passengers safe, stay alert, and take proactive actions to avoid the dangers posed by inclement weather changes.

These are just some of the key rules of safe boat operation. For more information, check out the United States Coast Guard's website listing boating safety courses available for all types of recreational boaters.

Notes:

Important things to consider when there's been a commercial or private boating accident: Was the boat properly manned? (Was the staff adequately trained? Was the operator under the influence of alcohol or drugs at the time of the incident?) Was the boat properly maintained? Was it fitted with required safety equipment?

Indiana Bicycle Safety Laws

"I heard that the Indiana General Assembly recently updated laws on bicycle safety and e-bike operation. What do I need to know?"

How many times have you encountered a bicyclist traveling in your lane of travel along the right side of the road? The bicyclist is not taking up the whole lane, but they are traveling pretty slowly in comparison to your vehicle and you want to try to get around them. However, with a steady stream of traffic in the other lanes around you, you have no safe way to go around the bicycle, and so you are stuck behind it, creeping along slowly.

As you look for traffic in the lanes around you to clear so that you can pass the bicyclist, you realize the coast is now clear and so you make your way around the bicyclist, careful to leave a few feet between you and them. But just how many feet of clearance should you leave between your vehicle and the bicyclist in order to safely pass them?

The answer is at least 3 feet, according to the Indiana state legislature.

Among the several new laws recently implemented in Indiana in 2019 is the new law for motorists to give at least 3 feet of clearance between their vehicle and a bicyclist when overtaking a bicycle that is proceeding in the same direction of travel.

Likewise, a motorist should only return to their original lane when it is evident that the bicyclist has safely been passed.

In addition to enacting the new "Give 3 Feet" law, governing the practice of safely overtaking a bicycle on the road in Indiana, the state has also acknowledged the increased use of electric bicycles by passing new classification laws and requirements regarding the use of electric bicycles.

So what is an electric bike?

An electric bike, also known as an e-bike, is a bicycle that has an electric motor to assist the operator in reaching top speeds of 20 to 28 mph. The motor shuts off when the cyclist either stops pedaling or applies the brakes. Electric bicycles have risen in popularity in recent years, particularly among those who use bicycles in their daily commute.

In Indiana, users of e-bikes have the same legal duties, rights, and privileges as bicycle operators.

The state categorizes electric bicycles into three classes. Class 1 e-bikes are those with motors that provide assistance only when the cyclist is pedaling and only functions until the e-bike reaches the top speed of 20 mph. Class 2 e-bikes are those with motors that can be used exclusively to propel the bicycle forward, without any pedaling from the cyclist. These have a top speed of 20 mph, at which point the motor will stop. Class 3 e-bikes are just like Class 1 e-bikes, except their top speed is 28 mph.

Generally speaking, electric bicycles can be ridden anywhere ordinary bicycles can be. However, those electric bicycles that can reach top speeds of 28 mph are not necessarily permitted on bike paths or sidewalks— but local ordinances and signs on particular paths can note if they are allowed. Some other special rules for the e-bikes that can go up to 28 mph include prohibiting those under the age of 15 from operating them.

For more detailed information on the new e-bike and bicyclist laws in Indiana, visit the Indiana General Assembly's webpage at http://www.iga.in.gov

Notes:

All states have "safe passing laws" requiring vehicles to pass bicyclists at a safe distance, but they don't all specify what distance is required for safe passing. Indiana has now joined with the majority of states requiring drivers to give at least 3 feet of road when passing a bicyclist.

Holub

Chapter 8

Hiring a Lawyer

Attorney Board Certification

"My doctors are board certified. Can attorneys also be board certified?"

Many people know that when choosing a doctor it's important to see if the doctor is board certified. However, when choosing an attorney, some people may not be aware of additional credentials that an attorney may obtain, such as becoming board certified in a particular area of law.

The attorney board certification process is similar to the medical board certification process. However, very few attorneys take the time to qualify to be board certified, or meet the rigorous qualification criteria.

For example, to qualify for board certification in civil trial advocacy, an attorney must meet the following criteria:

First, the attorney-applicant must prove that he or she substantially participated in at least forty-five days of trial during which the attorney examined or cross-examined witnesses, delivered an opening statement or closing argument or conducted a *voir dire* jury examination. During these forty-five or more trial days the attorney-applicant must personally have:

1. served as *lead* counsel in at least five jury cases;
2. *substantially participated* in at least five jury cases which have proceeded to verdict;
3. conducted *direct* examination of at least twenty-five lay witnesses;
4. conducted *cross*-examination of at least twenty-five lay witnesses;
5. conducted *direct* examination of at least fifteen expert witnesses;

6. conducted *cross*-examination of at least fifteen expert witnesses;
7. presented at least eight *opening statements*;
8. presented at least four *closing* arguments;
9. conducted at least five *voir dire* jury examinations

Second, the attorney-applicant must show that he or she actively participated in one hundred additional contested matters that involved the taking of testimony under oath, including participating in trials, evidentiary hearings, and depositions.

There are several other similar criteria that an attorney-applicant must meet to qualify for board certification, but you get the picture. The attorney must prove he or she has meaningful, practical trial experience.

Plus, there is also a multi-day written examination that the attorney must pass in order to become board certified.

Notes:

David Holub, the senior member of our firm, first acquired board certification in 1996, and continues to try many jury trials each year, both large and small.

Don't Hire a Fake Lawyer

"I hired a law firm and found out later that it was a fake law firm. What can people do to avoid being scammed by a fake lawyer through a fake website?"

Unfortunately, fake lawyers are becoming a problem across the United States.

Several times a week, we get people calling us about being ripped off by a fake lawyer or law firm. Yes, fake.

Apparently through the power of cut-and-paste websites these wannabe lawyers have convinced people to hire them. One woman said she shelled out hundreds of dollars just to tell her story. And, they wanted even more money to start her claim.

Another man revealed he had given someone he thought was a real attorney, his credit card number only to be swindled out of thousands of dollars. He then had to spend countless hours trying to rescind all the bogus charges racked up on his card.

On another occasion, a person said the firm they had thought they "hired" had the name of a once legit firm out of New York that had filed bankruptcy, so she thought the person she hired was a legitimate attorney. She had lots of phone calls with people at the firm, but never signed anything.

You might be thinking, "Why didn't these people do their due diligence? Why didn't they check these attorneys out?"

From experience, we can tell you that when we receive a call from someone who has been injured, they are not thinking as a cautious person would think. For the most part their guard is down.

They are looking for answers. They want direction. They think that if a person has a website they must be legitimate.

They want to hear that someone is going to help them, represent them, and defend them. They want to know that the person will be there every step of the way.

Sadly, if the person they are calling gives them that sense of security, that everything is going to be alright, it makes it easier for the scam to occur.

Look up the definition of the word grifter. These fake law firms prey upon people and gain their confidence.

The fact is that people rarely ever look for an attorney unless they are facing some crisis, injury or injustice. Unfortunately, by the time they are looking for any attorney they are in panic mode, scrambling to find someone.

In some areas of the United States the amount of phony legal firms being reported is almost one a day. So how do these scammers do it? How do they convince people to call them?

These con artists create bogus websites filled with copied images, slogans and even names of real lawyers to lend credibility. Some of these sites have mirrored articles, cases, and even testimonials off of real law firm sites to add to the illusion of being a legitimate firm.

So how do these fake lawyers make money? Well, these scammers require up-front funds. They state these fees are for processing your case, administrative work, or the cost to pull your file.

But once they get the money, they come up with excuse after excuse why your case has slowed down or they just don't return your calls at all.

Here are 8 tips to avoid being taken by a fake law firm:

1. Meet your lawyer in person at their office. Offices are harder to fake then websites.

2. Never pay an attorney online or over the phone.

3. Ask around. Get a referral from someone you know and trust.

4. Dive deep into the prospective lawyer's online reputation and notice inconsistencies. For example, our office has over 100 videos on YouTube and more videos on our website. We also have a podcast. We are everywhere! Duplicating that kind of a web presence and online reputation would be costly and extremely difficult.

5. Ask a lot of questions and seek out answers that make sense.

6. Hire a board certified civil trial attorney.

7. Look for an attorney with an honest and ethical reputation.

8. Select a lawyer who can explain the law to you in a clear and concise manner. A fake attorney isn't likely able to explain the law.

When it comes time to select the right attorney for your needs, you need to have the knowledge to choose wisely and get the absolute best representation for your case. First and foremost, we believe that hiring an attorney should be a matter of trust.

Notes:

Watch out for fake lawyers and law firms. Choose an attorney that you trust. Our clients know that we are here for them, fighting for them, educating them, and keeping them in the loop throughout the legal process.

Accessing Our Website

"Your website has a tremendous amount of information. What is the best way to access DavidHolubLaw.com to get the most out of the website?"

Our website www.DavidHolubLaw.com is filled with helpful information and we don't want you to miss out on any of it. Here's a simplified explanation of both the desktop and mobile versions of our website.

Desktop Version of Our Website

Along the top of our website are various title fields that can be used to navigate to different areas of interest.

Practice Areas – links to more detailed pages on the types of cases we handle.

Our Team – introduces you to the people who are part of the David Holub Law team and links to our reviews and testimonials.

Videos – links to all of our informational videos organized by topic area. Another great way to access our videos is via YouTube. Our YouTube page is linked at the bottom right of every page on our website or just search for David Holub Law on YouTube. You'll find our more than 100 videos very easily.

Links – connects you to many helpful legal resources. You'll also find "service" links to the many charity and service organizations supported by the David Holub Law team.

Blog – contains the hundreds of blog posts we've written on various aspects of personal injury law.

Notable Cases – highlights a number of the more noteworthy cases we have handled. While every case is important, many of these cases are unusual and worth spending a few moments to review.

In the middle of the home page of our website is a welcome video that tells you about our office and how we operate.

On the left side of every page on our website are three wide buttons to get quick guidance and learn about the factors you should consider when you are selecting an attorney to assist you.

Further down the left side of every page are more links to our practice areas.

In the middle and to the right of every page on our website, you'll find the *Quick Contact* box. This is where most people send us questions. You can get your podcast questions to us using this app.

On the bottom left of every webpage is *Site Map* which provides navigation similar to what's at the top of our webpage. However, it also contains our *Search Site* link, which is incredibly helpful for finding ANYTHING posted on our site.

Also, on the bottom middle of each page is a sign-up field to subscribe to our monthly e-newsletter. You can subscribe and unsubscribe very easily.

Oh, and at the top corner left of each page is a blue circled stick-figure icon. This is an accessibility menu for people who have vision difficulties. You can adjust the color contrast settings and type size, as well as have the page read to you.

Mobile Version of Our Website

For mobile users, clicking on the "hamburger" icon at the top of the page gets you to all of the top navigation links discussed earlier.

Scrolling down the page shows the links to the *Practice Area*s.

Scroll down further and you can see the blog post that we are highlighting for the week, as well as our welcome video.

Keep scrolling and you'll find the *Quick Contact* box.

Scroll further down and you'll see our testimonials.

There is also a link to *text us*, and a *live chat* link on each page.

Near the bottom of each page is the *Search Site* link.

So, there you have, in a nutshell, tips on how to navigate our website.

Holub

Chapter 9

General Case Tips

Police Reports

"A car knocked me down in a parking lot. No police came to make a report because I didn't think I was hurt, but now I am hurting and the bills are mounting. What are my legal options?"

First, it's not uncommon to suffer a trauma that initially appears to be minor, but that turns out to be a significant injury. Most doctors tell us that it can take as much as two weeks for injuries to appear following a trauma to the body. Quite often, people who suffer a trauma may initially think they are okay and not see a need to call the police or document the incident.

However, obtaining a police report in order to document an incident, even when it's not clear that you are hurt, is important. And, it's what we recommend. If you end up not being hurt, then you've just wasted a few minutes talking to a police officer, getting the name of the other party involved, as well as the name of the insurance company for the other party involved.

On the other hand, if you wind up being hurt, you'll be glad you took the extra few minutes to get a police report. But what if you are injured and you do not have a police report about the incident? Well, even if there is no police report, you still may be able to make a case.

We have found that with the low cost of security cameras in many parking lots for grocery stores, gas stations, pharmacies, shopping centers, and the like, there often may be retrievable video footage showing an injury incident, such as a knockdown of a pedestrian. Although the video quality is not always great, it can be good enough to allow an attorney to track down the party responsible for an injury.

For example, sometimes it's possible to see a license plate on a video. But even if there's not obviously identifying information in the video, there typically is a time and date stamp on a video, which alone can be used to try to identify parties. By knowing the date and time of an incident, it's possible to ask the business where the video footage was taken if there are retrievable records of transactions from that time period in question. Information from a credit card transaction can lead to the names of individuals who were present at the time of an incident.

So, the bottom line is that it is very important to get a police report, but all is not necessarily lost if you did not get one. Even your own purchase stub can help show the date and time of when you walked out of the store. That then can be cross-referenced against the cameras inside the store at the cash registers. Perhaps if your attorney obtains the video, when you watch the video you can identify the driver of the car standing in the checkout line before the incident. That, in turn, further narrows down the potential identity of who was involved in an injury incident.

Notes:

When in doubt, get a police report. Documenting an injury incident when it happens is always easier than trying to go back and piece things together later. Memories fade and video footage can be deleted.

Limited Time-Frame to File Suit

"How much time do I have before I am barred from bringing a lawsuit after I am injured in a motor vehicle crash or other incident?"

It is amazing the number of calls we get after the statute of limitations has expired to sue on a claim. It seems that the day-to-day necessities of life following a crash— such as traveling back and forth to the doctor, trying to work when you're not feeling well, going back and forth to get to physical therapy, and doing all the other things needed to recover—cause people to put off calling an attorney.

But, for a variety of reasons, that call to an attorney should not be delayed.

The law in Indiana is that a person injured in a crash, fall, or other incident, has to sue before the two year anniversary of the incident. In other words, the statute of limitations to file a lawsuit expires two years from the date the incident happened.

If you miss that deadline, then you can be barred from making a claim. There are some exceptions, so always check with an attorney even if you think it is too late to sue.

In addition to the general, two-year time frame rule, there are a whole host of other shorter limitation periods that can interfere with your ability to sue.

For example, a person generally only has 180 days from the date of an injury incident involving a governmental entity to file with the government a report called a tort claim notice. Those 180 days can go by very fast. We've had many people contact us after that deadline has expired. With very few exceptions, if no notice is given, then a person can't sue the government agency. Since there are a few exceptions though, you should always contact an attorney, even if you think it might be too late to proceed.

So, the bottom line is that to avoid these deadlines we would suggest that you either contact an attorney within a few days or weeks following an injury incident or note these important deadlines on your calendar right after an accident. These time-frame rules can easily slip your mind and the deadlines can creep up and bar your claim if you haven't sued or the other notice deadlines have passed.

Oh, and if you are thinking of calling an attorney the day before the time to sue expires, we would suggest that you re-think that. In such cases most attorneys will agree to file the case for you, but ask you to sign a disclaimer that you won't hold them responsible if a necessary party does not get named in the suit papers. Failing to name the correct party is just one of several things that can go wrong.

Notes:

When in doubt, talk with an attorney. Although there are time-frame rules about when a case can be brought, a good attorney may be able to advocate on your behalf that an exception to the time-frame rules applies in your situation.

Getting Property Damage Compensation

"I was recently in a collision and my car was totaled. How can I get the insurance company to pay for my property damage?"

In Indiana, if your vehicle sustains property damage as a result of a collision, there are potentially several options for getting compensation for that property damage.

First, you can check to see if your own automobile insurance policy provides collision coverage. Often this coverage is available to cover property damage that your vehicle sustained in a collision without any determination as to who was at fault for the collision. If you do have this type of coverage under your policy, you usually have to pay out your deductible amount in order to get the property damage compensation from your insurer. For example, if you have $5,000 worth of property damage and a $500 deductible, then your insurance would give you $4,500.

Second, if you don't have property damage coverage through your own automobile insurance policy, you can see if the other driver involved in the collision has insurance that will cover your property damage. However, you will not get anything from that other driver's insurance unless it is absolutely clear that the other driver was at fault for the collision. If it is clear that the other driver was at fault and that other driver's insurance company agrees, then you can get them to pay your property damage claim—and in such a situation there would be no deductible, so the insurer would pay your entire property damage claim.

Whether it's the other driver's insurer or your own that will pay your property damage claim, before that insurer pays you anything it is going to perform an analysis in which it determines the value of your vehicle, learns who has title to the vehicle, and other related information. It's a good idea to get a couple different estimates on your vehicle before you start talking with an adjuster from either party's insurance about the value of your vehicle.

Now if you were injured in the collision, you have to be very cautious about communicating with the other driver's insurance adjuster. Even if that insurance adjuster tells you that they're just solely dealing with property damage, anything you say about your injury or how you're feeling that day goes into their record and can be used against you when it comes to your bodily injury claim. If you are injured in a collision, we suggest you see an attorney before you even begin to discuss or negotiate your property damage claim or discuss anything with the other driver's insurance company.

Another thing to keep in mind is that if your vehicle has to be in the shop for a few weeks getting repair work done, you may be entitled to get a rental car. It depends on if you have that kind of rental car coverage under your own insurance policy. And under certain circumstances, you may also get the other driver's insurance company to pay for you to have a rental car while repairs are being done on your car if the other driver is very clearly at fault for the collision. However, that is not always the case, nor is it always possible.

Notes:

If there is a dispute as to which driver is at fault, your best option is to deal with your own insurance carrier. Your carrier is required to pay you regardless of fault if you have collision protection coverage on the car.

Giving a Statement to Insurance

"I was just in a crash and now the insurance company wants a statement. Should I talk to their representative?"

The answer depends on one key fact—whose insurance company is asking you for a statement?

For example, if a person is in a car crash and there are two vehicles involved, there will be two insurance companies. There will be your own insurance company, the company which ensures your car, and the other driver's insurance company.

Let's focus first on your own insurance company. If your own insurance company calls you and wants to take your statement, 99% of the time you will have to comply with that request, because 99% of all insurance policies require, as a matter of contract, that you must cooperate and give a statement and explain what happened. So . . . in the case of your own insurance company, you have to give a statement.

However, you certainly have the right to consult an attorney before giving a statement, and you can even have your attorney be present while you give a statement.

If you don't cooperate with your own insurance company, you could jeopardize your coverage by breaching your insurance contract. This means the insurer could decline to perform its obligations under the insurance policy. So, you need to cooperate. But, consulting an attorney can be very important.

Why? Because most auto insurance policies have different benefit tracks. For example, the policy will protect you against a liability claim for which you were at fault.

But the same policy may provide a coverage benefit called underinsured or uninsured motorist coverage. Such coverage means that if the person who hit you has no insurance or inadequate insurance, then your own insurance company will have an obligation to stand in the shoes of the other driver and may potentially owe you money for your injuries. This creates an adversarial relationship between you and your own insurance company. Consulting an attorney in an underinsured/uninsured motorist situation is very important.

Now let's focus on the other driver's insurance company for a moment. The other driver's insurance company is not even remotely your friend. It is your adversary.

The other driver's insurance company will do everything possible to minimize your claim and trick you and trap you into saying things that can be very harmful when you talk with them.

For example, they might ask you, "How are you doing today?" If you say, "fine," they will write down that you're not hurt and reported doing fine.

When the other driver's insurance company representatives want to speak to you, 99% of the time you would do well to consult an attorney before speaking to them.

Keep in mind you absolutely do not have to speak to an insurance representative who works for the company who insures the other driver. Sometimes, though, after a consult with an attorney, your attorney may decide that it makes sense to provide a limited statement about what happened. If so, the attorney will likely participate in any statement you give and object when necessary to protect you and limit your answers.

Dressing for a Deposition, Mediation, or Trial

"Why is it important to dress attractively for a deposition, mediation, or trial?"

Easy answer: respect. Each party in a relationship needs to feel respected by the other parties. But what does that have to do with an attorney talking to you about how to dress for legal proceedings?

Well, how we dress communicates a lot about us. If you dress nicely when you go into a courtroom, then you are communicating through your dress that you have respect for the judge, jury, witnesses, and everyone else in attendance.

What if you step into a courtroom wearing a burlap sack with a belt around the waist? What message would that send, especially compared to you stepping into the courtroom wearing clean, dark-colored, well-pressed pants or slacks, and a clean, buttoned-down, white or light-blue shirt or blouse?

Dressing nicely doesn't require very much effort, but the payoff can be very large.

The way we dress and present ourselves—from the way we comb our hair, to the presence of visible tattoos, to the type of jewelry we wear—all of it makes a huge difference and sends a signal to other people.

We are not trying to oppress someone when we talk about dressing nicely. We simply know that impressions are made by the way someone dresses and want you to have the best chance for making a good impression and showing respect for the legal process. If you're going for a job interview, then you're going to dress for the type of job that you are seeking. It's the same with legal proceedings.

Preparing for a Deposition

"Your office called to have me prepare for my deposition. What is the big deal? Is my deposition really that important?"

Many times a personal injury case client will ask, "Is my deposition really that important?" The answer is yes, but only if you want to win.

A deposition is a statement under oath taken down by a court reporter.

Yes, preparing for a deposition is a bit of a pain. To properly prepare you need to review the facts of your case with your attorney so that your memory is refreshed and you can answer accurately.

Answering deposition questions posed by the attorney for the other team is difficult and requires thoughtful consideration of the question before it is answered.

In other words, you don't get points for answering quickly or answering before you have listened to the entire question. The game is won by thinking before answering and by not providing information that was not asked. In other words, if you are asked, "Do you know what the date is today?" The answer should be "yes" or "no," not a response that actually provides the date.

Through it all, the overriding most important part of a deposition is really simple: tell the truth.

Witnesses are obliged to tell the truth, even when they think the truth will hurt their case. Often a truth that a client might think will hurt his or her case, does not at all hurt the case.

For example, if the "truth" of your past medical history in a case involving a broken leg is that ten years ago you broke the same leg, it is not damaging to your case to admit that fact.

Rather, the biggest mistake of all is to deny such a fact. Why? Because records will easily show that the denial was either a mistake or a lie. Mistakes can hurt you at trial, but lies can kill you at trial.

All things considered, a deposition is fairly easy as long as you don't get rattled or upset by the questions posed. If you prepare and go over things with your attorney beforehand, you will not be rattled or get upset. If you follow the advice of your attorney, you will do well. You will make a good impression on the defense attorney, who will be reporting back to the people who decide if they will settle with you or if they want to go to trial against you.

Notes:

Taking the time to prepare for your deposition is important. Don't worry about handling objections during the deposition – your lawyer may object to certain questions asked by the defense attorney, but that is your attorney's job, not your job. Your job is to answer truthfully.

Tips about Medical Treatment

"Since I got hurt, I'm either at the doctor's office or spending all my time and money getting prescribed treatment. Do you have any advice on how to deal with the frustrations I am experiencing?"

Without a doubt, an injury event will, in many respects, turn your life upside-down.

Before an accident, maybe you saw your doctor once a year for an annual physical, but now you find yourself at the doctor's office multiple times a month, driving to and from the doctor's office, going to imaging centers for tests, going to physical therapy, getting scheduled for surgery. . . the list goes on and on.

It can all be very frustrating. We get it. Although there are no statistical studies to back up the following advice, we have watched our many clients deal with these frustrations over the years and here are our observations.

First, if you're satisfied with your doctor, and think that he or she is providing you with sound advice, then following that advice is the best medicine. If you don't trust your current doctor, then seek out one you feel you can trust.

Second, we have found that people who do best on the road to recovery are those who work hard to communicate well with their doctors about their feelings, symptoms, pain levels, and progress with different exercises and activities.

Third, we also have found that treating your doctor with respect, including all of his or her staff members, can really help get the most out of medical care.

People who provide medical care for the most part genuinely want to help those who they have the ability to help.

Nothing makes a doctor or therapist more frustrated than to have a patient that fails to show up on time, misses appointments completely without explanation, or just simply refuses to follow the doctor's instructions.

Physicians are people too. If they do you a favor and get you in for an early appointment, then thank them. If one of their staff members goes out of their way to reschedule you at a more convenient time, then thank him or her.

Fourth, we find from reading so many medical records, especially those from therapists who are unhappy because the patient failed to show up for visit, that medical providers can become angry with patients. For example, if a therapist has set aside 1 o'clock on a Tuesday afternoon to help a patient, and that patient is a no-show for the appointment, not only does it affect that therapist's pocketbook, it also means that the therapist couldn't help somebody else in that same time slot who might very much need to be helped, but had to be turned away.

Lastly, we have found that people tend to get the most out of their medical providers when they are as accurate as they can be about their symptoms and how they're feeling.

Those who downplay their pain in a very stoic manner really do not do themselves a service, because care providers need to know precisely how a person is feeling.

If you're feeling pain at a level 5 out of 10, but report that your pain is a 2 out of 10, then you're not being accurate.

Likewise, if you report level 4 out of 10 pain, when you're really feeling level 5 out of 10 pain, then you're not being accurate.

Doctors have tests that they can administer to determine if a patient is exaggerating, and if they believe a patient is exaggerating, it changes their entire attitude towards the patient. So being accurate is important in order to get the best care, and to recover as quickly as possible from an injury.

Social Media Affects Trial

"How can my social media posting impact the trial of my claim? Isn't what I post private?"

We live in an era in which millions of people are involved in online social networking and posting on social media accounts such as Facebook, Twitter, and Instagram. It seems like almost every week we're hearing about data breaches, privacy violations, and algorithmic manipulation affecting large numbers of people.

In addition to all of those concerning discoveries, it may come as no surprise that the personal data available via social networking platforms has profoundly impacted the legal field—altering trial techniques and practices. Your social media posts, and those you are tagged in, can have a direct impact on the value of your case and have the ability to undermine your credibility to a jury, if the posts are inconsistent with the injuries and complaints you are making.

You are probably familiar with the concept of surveillance and how, for years, insurance companies have utilized video surveillance to try to show that a person is lying about the severity of his or her injuries. You know, the situation in which someone complaining that their back pain is so severe that they can't work or do basic daily activities, such as doing laundry, is caught on camera dancing the night away at a friend's wedding.

Well, those same surveillance tactics that have been used in litigation for years are now being applied to the world of social media. New look, same tactic. Now, instead of hiring someone to follow you with a video camera to conduct surveillance, many insurance companies are performing all kinds of web searches on various social media platforms about you. They examine your Facebook, Twitter, and Instagram pages and profiles to see if there are any inconsistencies with your claimed injuries.

Although we find that our clients would never be involved in anything that is inconsistent with their injuries, it's important to just keep in mind that defendants and insurance companies look at all your social media pages and accounts.

It's our suggestion that during the time that you are recovering from any kind of injury incident, you refrain from posting anything about the incident or your injuries. It's even a good idea to suspend your use of social media accounts while your case is pending or when there is a *prospect* of a claim before a case has been filed.

While you are recovering from an injury, we recommend keeping a private journal noting how you're feeling and the doctor appointments you're attending (along with what the doctor tells you). These private journal entries can help refresh your memory in the future if there is a trial.

Notes:

After being injured in a crash or other incident, it can be tempting to want to upload photos of your wrecked vehicle and bruised up body to let your friends and family know about it, but resist the urge. Your photos and posts can be used by the defense to try to harm your case. The smartest move you can make is to proactively stop using your social media accounts after you've been in an injury event.

Holub

Chapter 10

Legal Concepts

Insurance Replacement Cost

"A storm ripped off the roof on my home. Will my storm damage insurance cover the cost to install a new roof?"

When people purchase insurance, they usually do so to protect themselves from catastrophic loss due to foreseeable, but relatively rare events.

Insurance companies love to take your premiums, but when it comes to paying money out on a loss, they too often look for every possible excuse to avoid paying you.

One issue that comes up with storm damage insurance is whether you can make an insurance company buy you a brand-new roof after a storm damages the roof, even if it was a 20-year old roof before the storm?

Our answer is that "it depends." If you purchase replacement cost coverage, usually the answer is yes. You pay extra for replacement cost coverage. The insurance company took your money, so it should have to pay whatever it costs to replace what the storm damaged.

But all too frequently, even though you purchase replacement cost coverage, you might hear the insurance company speak about depreciation and wear and tear deductions. If you hear such terms in response to a replacement cost claim, you need to promptly call an attorney. If you continue to talk to the insurance company on your own without an attorney, the odds are high that it will continue to try to take advantage of you.

If you buy replacement cost coverage for fire, and your place burns down and is a total loss, you should in most cases be able to make the insurance carrier pay to rebuild, even if it costs $250,000 to rebuild, and the house was only worth $25,000 on the open real estate market before the fire.

In total loss cases insurance companies know you're not going to listen to them talk about depreciation. Why? Because EVERYTHING needs to be replaced.

With roof storm damage, though, many companies try to get away with talking about wear and tear and depreciation because usually only a portion of the roof is missing. If, in such a case, an insurance company says, "We'll patch the roof at whatever it costs to replace the damaged portion," then it somewhat sounds plausible to many homeowners. However, if you paid for replacement coverage, then you should get it.

A house with a patchwork roof—with new colored shingles in one area and a different old-looking area of shingles in another area—is not going to sell for the same amount as a house with a single uniform-colored roof with matching shingles. So, in most cases, unless there is unusual wording in the policy, replacement cost under the law should entitle the homeowner to replacement of the entire roof. Not just a patched-up roof.

Multi-District Litigation

"What is multi-district litigation?"

There is an area of the law referred to as complex litigation. It is a catch-all umbrella term that encompasses class actions, and includes multi-district litigation.

Multi-district litigation, sometimes referred to by the abbreviation MDL, is a litigation management tool used by the federal courts to streamline the management of complex litigation.

When courts were confronted with class action lawsuits popping up in different areas of the country—large groups of people scattered across a vast geographic area all bringing similar claims against the same party or parties—the courts had to come up with a way to effectively and efficiently manage all of those similar cases.

Consider the following example to illustrate the picture: Let's say a company sells a cleaning chemical called Spiffy-Clean. Suppose the workers who used Spiffy-Clean start showing up to their doctors with cancer. They then get attorneys, and all of the workers who used Spiffy-Clean sue the maker of Spiffy-Clean for its defective product, claiming a lack of warning.

A key issue in a product liability cleaning chemical case, such as the one involving the make-believe product Spiffy-Clean, is whether the chemical manufacturer knew that the cleaning chemical product was carcinogenic.

Let's say that when the workers who used Spiffy-Clean file suit, they file 150 individual lawsuits across the country. While the case is pending, suppose each of the workers' attorneys wishes to question under oath Spiffy-Clean's director of research. Without an MDL court to manage all of these 150 cases under one umbrella, Spiffy-Clean's director of research will have to be questioned under oath 150 times. In contrast, under the management of an MDL court, the director of research will only be questioned under oath one time.

So how exactly does MDL work?

Typically, in an MDL situation, rather than having each individual plaintiff's attorney operating separately, a committee of attorneys acts together throughout the case to streamline the logistics. For example, a committee of plaintiff's attorneys may dedicate their efforts to tackle a particular aspect of the case together, such as taking the deposition of the head of Spiffy-Clean's manufacturing division.

In such a case, a group of plaintiff's attorneys working together organize the work load and decide what questions to ask, and who is going to ask the questions.

A similar committee might be formed about experts on the health impact of Spiffy-Clean.

So instead of 150 battles about the same issue going on all over the country there's only one battle, and the MDL court decides how that issue will proceed and whether the experts can testify and what they can say before a jury.

Thus, in multidistrict litigation, the multiple civil cases that share a common issue are transferred to a single district court. That court handles all discovery and pretrial proceedings of a case. If a case does not settle during MDL, it is typically sent back to the court in which the claim was originally brought for trial.

Having one court manage what goes on in multiple similar cases has worked very well in the cases in which our office has been involved.

One such case involved contaminated injections that were provided to multiple patients. The injections were contaminated with a fungus. The injections killed several people and injured many others in multiple states. Although that particular case functioned like an

MDL, it was managed by a bankruptcy judge because the manufacturer of the product filed for bankruptcy court protection because there were far more claims than available assets to pay all of the claims.

Notes:

In short, MDL is an effective, organized way for the courts to manage multiple class actions at once and simplify the legal process in such cases.

Comparative Fault and Recoverable Damages

"Can I recover compensation for an injury, even if I was partly at fault?"

It is possible to recover compensation for your injuries even if you were partly at fault, but only as long as you were not more than 50% at fault.

A motor vehicle crash or other injury incident often occurs because of a number of reasons, as opposed to a single reason. Injuries can happen due to shared fault on the part of the several parties involved in the incident, including the person who winds up injured.

If you're concerned that you cannot be compensated for your injury because you might share some fault for the injury incident, then you need to call an attorney to discuss the matter in detail. Things may not be as cut and dry as you think. Meeting with an attorney and discussing exactly what happened may reveal that, although you may have been partly at fault for your injury occurring, your percentage of fault is not substantial to block legal avenues for compensation for your injury.

Here's the way the law in Indiana works: if you are mostly at fault, meaning over 50% at fault, then Indiana law says you can't receive compensation for your injury.

But, that means that you have to be proven by the other party to be mostly at fault. The other party has the burden of proving you share fault, and a lot goes into proving that. What if the other party doesn't have evidence of your fault, or doesn't even think you share fault?

You might think on the surface that it's easy to prove who is at fault for a crash, but a lot of times evidence cuts both ways.

If the other party is mostly at fault, but you are somewhat at fault, you can recover. However, you only can recover for the percentage of fault that the other party is found to have contributed to cause the injury incident.

For example if the other party is 52% at fault, and a jury awards $100,000 in damages, you only recover $52,000.

Suppose that two cars crash in an intersection in which the traffic lights are out because of a power outage. In that situation, both cars are supposed to stop and treat the intersection as a four-way stop.

Now suppose that the evidence shows that the light went out only seconds before the crash. In that case, people on one side of the intersection were looking at a red light, and people on the other side were seeing a green or a yellow light.

Suppose further that your light was green when you last looked up a split second before the crash, and that when you looked back at the road you were never even aware that the power went out before you felt the impact. Under such a scenario, a jury might well see the other party as mostly responsible for the crash.

Notes:

The bottom line is that you need to have an experienced attorney help you sort things out. Until you speak with an attorney you should not assume that your situation is hopeless, even if you think you might be partly at fault.

Polygraph Tests

"I want to sue my neighbor for backing into my parked car. I know he did it, even though I have no evidence. Can't we just make him take a polygraph and use that as proof?"

Great question. Unfortunately, the answer is no.

TV legal drama programs often use lie detectors. Federal agents must, in certain internal security matters, submit to polygraphs. But, in most civil case situations you cannot make someone take a polygraph.

There are some employment contract situations in which people, as a condition of employment, agree to submit to lie detectors and agree that employment decisions can be made using test results. However, these kinds of situations are typically limited to high security businesses.

Generally speaking, courts don't rely on or allow polygraph test results to be admitted into evidence. Why?

The prime reason is that the lie detector polygraph machine can't reliably distinguish between a truth and a lie.

A polygraph simply measures biological processes such as blood pressure and heart rate.

When hooked up to a lie detector, sensors are placed on your fingers, chest and forehead in order to monitor your body's physical response to certain questions.

Usually the test operator starts off with basic questions, such as asking your name, where you live, your occupation. These questions are supposed to create a baseline, which will be used to compare with your responses to additional questions.

The test operator then usually starts asking some more challenging questions, which are designed to get you to review detailed answers or to create confusion.

When the needle measuring your response goes wild, the operator makes a note on the readings, indicating that you may have lied, felt pressured, or nervous.

The machine records your nervousness, sweating, and even temperature changes on your skin.

Do these physical responses mean that you lied? Not necessarily. Maybe you were nervous being hooked up to a machine or being scrutinized in that fashion, but now the machine shows you guilty of a lie. See the problem?

If you truly believe something to be true or your memory has been manipulated, then nothing you say will be considered a lie by the machine because your blood pressure or heart rate will not spike. The lie detector will show signs of you being truthful. Now you're probably thinking, "How can someone be manipulated?"

Memory is pliable. Memories can be altered, details added later, and some events totally fabricated in our minds.

People under hypnosis, for example, can be implanted with false memories. They recall events as if they were there in that moment, yet the event never really happened. And people who suffer traumatic experiences (injuries, assaults, accidents, war) may create false memories to protect themselves, to shield themselves from remembering what actually happened.

In a newspaper commentary in 2018, a writer pointed to a study where it was relatively easy to "implant" false memories in a significant number of lab subjects by showing them an official-looking poster of Disney characters, including Mickey Mouse and Bugs Bunny. When questioned later, many subjects remembered meeting Bugs Bunny on a childhood trip to Disneyland. Some even reported that Bugs had touched them inappropriately. However, those "memories" could not possibly be true because Bugs Bunny is not a Disney character.

When it comes down to memory recall, a person able to share more vivid, more detailed memories might be considered by others to be more credible and truthful, even if that person is actually lying, than a person who remembers only a few facts. If lawyers, judges, or juries made decisions based solely on the recall of someone's memory, the one who remembers the most would win every time, regardless of whether their statements were really the truth.

Notes:

Evidence is important. Specifically, physical evidence—things like footprints, DNA, and fingerprints—is important. Physical evidence can be more reliable than memories.

Holub

Chapter 11

Miscellaneous

Proving an Email Was Sent

"I sent an email to my insurance carrier to add a new car for coverage, but they claim they never received it and won't cover the damage sustained in the crash. What can I do?"

Historically, contract law governs business dealings. But in this technological age, it has been found lacking. So, the National Conference of Commissioners on Uniform State Laws wrote a model act called the Uniform Electronic Transactions Act (UETA) to govern transactions conducted via email over the internet.

Many states have adopted the UETA, including Indiana. The UETA was designed, in particular, to remove barriers to electronic commerce by validating and providing a clear framework for electronic records, signatures, and contracts as it pertains to people and businesses that have agreed to conduct business electronically.

As models for doing business have evolved to incorporate the speed, efficiencies, and financial savings offered by electronic technologies, the government has realized it does not want to stand in the way of such valuable economic potential, yet it does want to ensure that certain legal requirements are spelled out in order to bring certainty and consistency to e-commerce.

People and businesses conduct all kinds of transactions electronically these days, and e-commerce will only continue to expand in future years. Whether you've purchased something through the internet, completed an online banking transaction, signed e-documents by checking a box on a computer, or communicated to your healthcare provider through an online messaging portal, you've likely benefited from the convenience of e-commerce in one way or another.

When email is used for business purposes, then the UETA steps in and provides the ground rules for when an email will be considered "sent" and "received" by law.

Let's say you're arranging for a company to come and apply fertilizer and weed killer to your lawn. The company emails you its estimate for the job and you respond to the email saying that you want to go ahead and have them do the job for you. You send the company the money for the job, and you believe that it has come out and applied the fertilizer and weed killer. This would be an example of an electronic transaction covered under Indiana's UETA.

Now let's say you paid the fertilizer company, but later find out that it did not actually do the job—and it claims it never received your email in response to their emailed estimate. What does the law have to say about whether your email was actually sent and received?

Well, under Indiana's UETA, an email is considered to be sent when it enters a processing system outside of the sender's control in a properly addressed format. Similarly, an email is considered to be received when it enters a recipient's processing system. Importantly, the law specifically notes that a recipient's lack of awareness of receipt has no bearing on whether an email is legally deemed to have been received.

As you may know, when someone sends an email, it first must leave the sender's Message Transfer Agent (MTA) and then it begins the routing process through the network from one MTA to another until it reaches the recipient's mail server. After it leaves the sender's MTA and is in the hop-to-hop routing process, if an error occurs at any point through the various MTAs, then a bounce message is automatically generated and sent to the sender notifying of a delivery failure.

So in our example, if you sent an email to the fertilizer company that was properly addressed and you did not get an error message after you sent it (assuming you had an internet connection and it truly left your MTA and began the delivery routing process), then by law, that

131

email is deemed sent because it left your MTA—it entered a processing system outside of the email sender's control. Furthermore, the law would deem it to be successfully received by the recipient, even if the recipient was unaware of it, since no delivery error message was generated as the email went through the delivery process and finally entered a processing system within the recipient's control.

The comments to the UETA, which show the drafters' intent, emphasize that the law is designed to bind the computer user, regardless of whether that human user actually looks at and reviews a particular email or electronic transaction. It is no different from how the law views a paper notice in someone's mailbox effectively received even if the recipient never actually opens and reads the mailed paper notice.

In a situation in which someone sends an email to their insurer to add a new car to their coverage, but the insurer doesn't add the car and later claims it never received the email request, proving that the email was really sent and received by the insurer is important and can be pivotal to finding coverage for that vehicle.

Notes:

Important things to look for in proving whether an email was sent and received: read-receipt, proof that *another* recipient received the email in question, lack of a delivery error message to the sender. If possible, save the sent email so that the meta-data on it is preserved and can be analyzed.

Online Stores Try To Avoid Liability

"I was injured by a defective product that I bought online. Can I sue the online store?"

Unfortunately, there is a growing number of people who are being harmed by products purchased online that are, unbeknownst to the customer, banned, unsafe, and/or mislabeled on the website.

For example, a 2019 investigation by the Wall Street Journal revealed that thousands of items for sale on Amazon.com have been declared unsafe by federal agencies, are deceptively labeled, or are banned by federal regulators to even be on the market. Many online products are listed in the product description as being DOT-compliant, FDA approved, or UL certified, when in fact, they are not. Additionally, some items such as children's toys, were purchased online and tested for toxicity, and showed that they contained dangerously high levels of lead.

Generally, when people buy goods at a brick-and-mortar store, the law places a responsibility on the store to only sell goods that are deemed safe for consumers. Say, for example, you purchase an item at a big box store and it turns out to be defective and injure you, the law typically allows you, the injured consumer, to hold not only the manufacturer of the item responsible for your injuries, but also the seller of that item—in other words, the big box store.

But what happens in the world of online shopping? Say you purchase a small kitchen appliance online that turns out to be defective and dangerous and injures you. Can you hold the online store responsible for selling you the item the same way you can hold a brick-and-mortar store responsible for selling a defective product? Well, the answer is a bit complicated, and the law appears to be slowly changing.

For example, was the item purchased directly from an online store's website or was it actually purchased from a third party seller that is hosted on the online store's website? Some online stores make it clear when a person is buying from a third party seller, but other times, it is anything but clear.

Many online stores, even those that originally started out as selling directly to consumers, have evolved into something more like a flea market where a large percentage of the products for sale are actually sold through third party sellers or vendors—many of whom can be anonymous. When online stores allow third party sellers to sell products on their website, it breaks the direct supply and distribution chain that typical brick-and-mortar stores have over their products. In other words, it breaks the direct chains of supply and distribution which the law has reasoned as an important basis for holding sellers responsible for selling defective and/or dangerous products.

It is important to point out that not all online stores are equal in how they allow third party sellers access to sell through their websites or in how they police third party sellers to only sell safe and genuine products. Some websites really vet their third party sellers, while others grant immediate access.

So why does this all matter? Well, if you or a loved one is injured or even killed by a defective or dangerous product that was purchased online, this may really impact your ability to hold an online retailer or seller liable for the damages. In an effort to avoid liability, many online retailers argue that they can't be held liable for the defective or dangerous product that harmed someone because they were not the actual seller, but rather, just an online platform hosting third party sellers. Many times, the third party sellers are individuals or small businesses that have no insurance or way to pay for causing harm to customers.

However, some courts, such as the Third Circuit U.S. Court of Appeals, are finding that online retailers may still be held liable even if a defective or dangerous product is sold by a third party seller because the online retailer has a responsibility to vet and control the third party sellers it allows to use its website.

Notes:

When shopping online, pay attention to whether you are purchasing from a third party seller that's being hosted on an online retailer's website or whether you are purchasing directly from the online retailer.

Traumatic Brain Injury Claims

"My child suffered a brain injury in a crash. The doctor described it as mild, but the symptoms are not mild—they seem to be terrible. Do I need a brain injury lawyer?"

Over the years we have counseled lots of people who have suffered what is often called a traumatic brain injury or TBI. Sometimes doctors describe an injury as a mild TBI. The term mild does not mean minor or inconsequential, but is usually meant to distinguish open head injuries or closed head injuries with internal bleeding, sometimes called a brain bleed. We have helped both people with mild TBI claims and major brain injury claims.

When you or a loved one is suffering the effects of a brain injury, is it important to hire a lawyer who is experienced in dealing with brain injury claims? Definitely YES.

The law for a brain injury or a head injury is the same as it is for other personal injury cases. But brain injury cases can be more costly to pursue because specialized expert testimony is often needed.

Insurance carriers frequently fight brain injury cases because they hope they can convince a jury that the injury is not real or that it is exaggerated. They typically do not want to acknowledge that the damages inflicted are quite serious and life-changing.

Even a simple rear-end motor vehicle collision can cause a concussion that leaves devastating symptoms. Just ask Clark Elliott, Ph.D., a scientist in the field of artificial intelligence, who wrote a book about his experience living with the debilitating effects of a concussion for eight years before he finally got help from two Chicago-area researchers-clinicians: one an optometrist using neuro-developmental techniques and the other a cognitive restructuring specialist working on brain plasticity. His book is entitled *The Ghost in My Brain: How a Concussion Stole My Life and How the New Science of Brain Plasticity Helped Me Get it Back.*

Traumatic brain injuries are the result of head trauma, broken down into open head injury (skull fracture), closed head injury (concussions, contusions, or intracranial hemorrhage), and a particular type of closed head injury common in rapid deceleration situations like vehicle crashes or sports injuries called diffuse axonal shearing.

The symptoms of a traumatic brain injury are linked to the seriousness of the injury and how much damage is suffered to brain tissue. There are three main types: mild, moderate, and severe.

A mild TBI usually results in minimal or no loss of consciousness, and the symptoms may include headaches, nausea, difficulty sleeping, dizziness, issues with balance, sensory overload, cognitive deficits (such as inability to concentrate, confusion, memory loss, difficulty with word recall, problems reading or writing), vision problems (including blurred vision, abnormal eye movements, poor eye coordination, sensitivity to light, seeing more in two dimensions rather than three, unable to judge distance very well), hearing issues (including sensitivity to sound, partial hearing loss, or ringing in the ears), changes in smell or taste (either increased or decreased sensitivities), physical changes of appetite, sleep, and hormones, and/or fatigue. Even a so-called "mild" TBI can have profound effects on all aspects of a person's life, including basic tasks of thinking and moving around in the environment. Once a brain has been switched into a fight-or-flight state of alertness and remains there for a great amount of time, life itself becomes overwhelming— with persistent heightened sensitivities to light, sound, and movement.

In a recent issue of JAMA Psychiatry, a study showed that one in five individuals who have sustained a mild head injury will develop mental health conditions, such as depressive disorder, personality changes, and/or behavioral abnormalities.

A moderate TBI has similar symptoms, but may also include a longer period of time being unconscious upon injury, seizures or convulsions, extreme headaches, and/or loss of coordination.

The worst of the symptoms are associated with a severe TBI, which often results in slurred speech, agitation, inability to awaken from sleep, weakness or numbness in extremities, or a coma.

Major brain injuries are not hard to diagnose. But, even if there is an open fracture, or clear evidence of injury, doctors need to rely on an MRI or CT scan to identify an intracranial hematoma, hemorrhage or other abnormalities. The degree of injury, however, whether mild or severe or in between, is often hard to diagnose, and doctors often rely on assessing how a patient performs at solving puzzles and other brain skills tests.

Doctors have learned to quantify symptoms and have developed something called the Glasgow Coma Scale which quantifies eye response, verbal response, and motor response on numerical scales from 1-6. Other tests are used to evaluate a patient's awareness, cognition, behavior, and interaction with the environment.

Recovery from a brain injury is possible, though even mild traumatic brain injuries can cause permanent damage from which the affected individual never fully recovers. Sometimes the symptoms are such that the brain injury victim is disabled by the injury and qualifies for Supplemental Security Income (SSI) or Social Security Disability Insurance (SSDI) benefits.

In recent years, we have put together a pamphlet for clients and their families that explain treatment options for TBIs. This is helpful for the injured person, as well as the family, and guides them to the many resources available for TBI victims. For too many years, TBI victims have been left as the walking wounded, with symptoms that are medically unverifiable and therefore untreatable. Now, with more studies and resources coming out about the new science of brain plasticity to rewire and retrain the brain, there is hope for TBI victims.

Notes:

It is key to have an attorney representing you who understands the intricacies and complexities of brain injuries in order to better advocate for you and plead your case.

Social Media Account Suspension

"My social media account was suspended. What are my legal options?"

Having a social media account suspended is not within the field of personal injury law directly. However, since we often advise people of the hazards of posting to social media while a lawsuit is pending, we'll look at the legal ramifications of having a social media account suspended.

Freedom of speech is a simple concept. Modern-day social media is little more than an electronic version of a traditional daily newspaper's letter-to-the-editor section which affords people the opportunity to state their opinions for free.

Of course, the social media platform makes money by permitting people to buy ads and intersperse those ads along a user's media time line. Pretty inventive way to make money isn't it?

Since the social media platform essentially owns the paper, ink, and printing press, the law permits the platform owner to decline to publish the opinions of those with whom he or she disagrees.

So, if your social media account is suspended is there nothing you can do?

Maybe not. But, since modern social media publishing piggy-backs off of radio signals owned by the public (enabling internet on your smartphone) couldn't the government step in and "regulate" and set strict criteria for blocking ideas not welcomed by the owner of a media site? Sure. But would government end up further restricting free speech?

On the one hand, the legislature could craft a statute that only allows social media companies to limit a specific kind of speech, say, for example, speech explicitly calling for physical violence. However, enacting such a law could crack the door open for bureaucratic "regulators" to abuse their power and actually expand the definition of speech that could be suppressed. That is the slippery slope argument you often hear.

But, what about a law that, instead of regulating social media sites through an unwieldly government regulatory agency, simply permits a person who has their speech blocked for an illegitimate reason to sue in court for liquidated damages?

Liquidated damages are basically predetermined damages that can be obtained so as to eliminate the need to prove specific harm.

A law permitting liquidated damages might be very effective and would read something like:

> . . . any person who has been restricted in their freedom to post to a social media platform which utilizes public radio frequencies for any reason other than for speech explicitly calling for physical violence, may sue for an injunction to compel the unrestricted dissemination of such speech, as well as liquidated damages of $50,000.00 per day per violation.

Such a law would be self-enforcing. The person seeking to enforce the law would have to hire an attorney and spend money to pursue the remedy. But having to pay money to wrongly blocked users might make media sites hesitate to arbitrarily shut down a user's speech or shadow-ban his or her account.

As it stands, the Executive Order on Preventing Online Censorship issued by President Trump on May 28, 2020, sets forth that the Federal Communications Commission (FCC) shall promulgate rules that clarify existing statute—47 U.S.C. 230(c)—from the

Communications Decency Act. Under Section 230, interactive computer service providers receive immunity from civil liability when they act in "good faith" to remove content that is "obscene, lewd, lascivious, filthy, excessively violent, harassing or otherwise objectionable." 47 U.S.C. 230(c)(2).

President Trump's Executive Order requests that the FCC clarify what kind of content removal or restriction is encompassed within Section 230. The federal agency's rules are to make clear when a provider can and cannot claim immunity from civil liability in removing or restricting access to certain content. In other words, the new FCC rules will note when a provider has engaged in editorial conduct so as to expose itself to liability "like any traditional editor and publisher that is not an online provider."

The Order also describes investigative action that federal agencies will take to ensure that federal taxpayer dollars are not financing online platforms that restrict free speech. Furthermore, the Federal Trade Commission (FTC) will consider taking action under the law to prohibit online platforms such as Twitter, Facebook, and YouTube from engaging in unfair or deceptive acts or practices in or affecting commerce.

But what can people who fear being blocked legally do as a means of self-help right now? Here are some thoughts:

1. Social media opinion-maker stars who thrive on posting and who fear being blocked could buy their own modern-day newspaper. They could invest in their own domain name and make sure that name is widely known, and set up a website with a host that will not block them. Then if a block on a social media site occurs, a platform exists for their followers to seek them out.

2. Social media stars could be more social. They could follow-back all of their followers and encourage all of their followers to follow other followers. This could make it much more difficult to isolate people who are well

interconnected. Further, sharing of email addresses could make newsletter dissemination of opinions via email impossible to stop if a social media platform gets suspended.

School Shootings and Tort Law

"Is there a link between school shootings and personal injury law?"

The answer is yes, in part. Maybe in large part.

What makes schools soft targets for evil and demented people who go there to instigate their planned harm? Well, one reason is limited security coupled with potential victims who are unable to protect themselves.

But why is security so limited? Could the answer actually lie in the way the tort system has developed in this country? Yes.

Schools are agencies of the government. The government, in most states, largely makes itself immune from liability, or at the very least, severely limits damages recoverable when lawsuits are brought against governments for security failures.

The government does not have to pay the millions of dollars that would be owed by a private company with provable knowledge of major security risks, say to a concert venue or ballpark.

Consequently, there is little real pressure on governmental actors to make the necessary security decisions that could easily make schools safer places.

Incidentally, there are nearly no negative financial ramifications for officials who ignore signs that a potential murderer is mentally unbalanced. Likewise, there are basically no negative financial consequences for officials who decide not to act on or investigate reported concerns about an individual's instability.

Instead, there is a financial penalty if an official is overly-aggressive and wrongfully detains someone. However, such financial damages are limited in most jurisdictions as part of the governmental immunity laws.

So, if you are an official who is found to have made an error in asking for a judicial psych evaluation on someone, there is a price to pay. But if you don't act to stop a potentially dangerous person, there is no price. No financial price, that is.

If a government official is weighing the odds of adverse job repercussions, the odds always say (from a lawsuit danger perspective): ignore the warning signs.

Again, there is very little legal jeopardy for school administrators if they decide to look the other way and let violent actors get more and more violent. In contrast, there is potentially *great* legal jeopardy to be faced by administrators if they take action to clamp down on violent actors when the initial signs of violence are recognizable.

So unfortunately, we see time and time again that governmental agencies drop the ball on security because there are few employment or financial repercussions for dropping the ball.

Maybe a governmental agency fails to inspect scaffolding for safety code violations at a state fair and then that scaffolding winds up injuring or killing people, like what happened in Indiana a few years ago.

Or perhaps a governmental agency fails to require proper reconstruction of flood levies that were mistakenly torn down, like what happened in a case we litigated dozens of years ago.

The lack of financial accountability for governmental agencies leads to poor decisions by government officials. It is human nature for an official to worry about his or her job more than public safety.

So, when you hear politicians run to a microphone and talk about making laws that deal with whatever instrument bad people might want to use to create mayhem, whether it be IEDs, cars mowing down pedestrians, or firearms, is it all just talk?

Is it all to give the impression of solving a problem without really solving it?

To really stop school shootings, a careful systematic assessment needs to be done to make sure all decision points for governmental officials charged with making security decisions make the interests of the children paramount.

Maybe that means having off-duty police officers at every school. Maybe it means something different. But, things can and should be done to make children safe.

We just have to have the collective will to recognize the problem, and then to fix the problem.

Suing a Friend

"What happens if the person who injured me is a friend? Will suing my friend lead to the end of our friendship?"

In this day and age, getting unfriended on social media is a frequent occurrence. But what happens if the person who injured you is a real friend? If you file suit against a friend will your friendship end?

One of the most watched videos on our YouTube page —"Is It Ever Proper to Sue a Friend?"—explains why the odds are great that the person you might have to sue will be a friend or even a relative.

Think about it. Who do you hang out with more— friends or strangers? If you are like most people you spend your time with friends. That means you might be in a car with a friend or you might be on the property of a friend.

Consider a fall injury. Sure, you might fall at a restaurant or a store. But, quite frequently, people who get hurt on someone's property actually get hurt on the property of people they know.

How often do you trespass onto the property of a stranger?

If you think about it, people who buy insurance actually buy insurance not only to protect themselves against a judgment if a stranger might sue them, they buy insurance to protect their friends and relatives that come onto their property. Why? Because those people are the ones who are likely to be injured coming onto the property. 90% of the time people coming onto your property are people that you know.

But does suing a friend necessarily mean the end of a friendship? No!

It's normal to be apprehensive about making a claim against someone that you know—whether they're a friend or simply an acquaintance.

Say you're a passenger in your brother-in-law's car and he drives like a maniac and flips the car and you're seriously injured. What if you hire an attorney and the attorney gives notice to your brother-in-law's insurance company and the insurance company contacts the brother-in-law? Now all of a sudden, you've got an irate family member wondering if you're suing them and if it will jeopardize their finances beyond their insurance coverage amount.

If this is a concern of yours, are there things that you and your attorney can do to avoid this type of rift in a relationship? Sure. There are lots of things.

One, you can ask your attorney to guard against the potential for hard feelings by writing to the friend or relative that you may need to sue and telling them that you will only be going after their insurance or that you will not, in any way, attempt to take their car, home, or other assets.

Two, you can ask your attorney to call and explain the same thing to your friend or relative. Attorneys are prohibited from contacting and speaking with someone who is already represented by an attorney, but if your friend or relative is not represented by an attorney, then there is no reason why your attorney can't call and explain what your view is and how you anticipate only going after their insurance.

Do these things always work to smooth over hard feelings and prevent damage to a relationship? Yeah—most of the time they do.

Now sometimes it may take some work by your attorney to get through to a friend or relative that you're only interested in obtaining insurance to cover medical bills and lost time from work. But in most cases, people understand and are not mad once it's explained to them and they're approached in the right way.

Notes:

We understand a person may initially be apprehensive to sue a friend or relative after being injured, but once your attorney explains to the friend or relative the situation and that you will only be going after their insurance, most people are accepting and not mad.

Holub

About the Authors

David W. Holub was admitted to practice before the Indiana State and U.S. Federal District Courts, Southern and Northern Districts of Indiana in 1982. He was admitted to practice before the Supreme Court of the United States in 1995. He is also admitted to practice before the U.S. Federal District Court in the Northern District of Illinois, and the U.S. Court of Appeals for the Seventh Circuit.

Education: Olivet College (B.A. Magna Cum Laude, 1979); Valparaiso University (J.D. 1982). Associate Editor, Valparaiso University Law Review, 1981-1982.

Publications and Presentations:

- Speaker, Insurance Coverage Litigation: Secrets Insurance Companies Don't Want Attorneys to Know (NBI, December, 2019).
- Speaker, Civil Trial: Everything You Need to Know (NBI, August, 2019).
- Speaker, Civil Trial From Start to Finish (NBI, December, 2018).
- Author, Fighting For Truth: A Trial Lawyer's Insight Into What It Takes To Win Amazon (July, 2018).
- Seminar Moderator, What Civil Court Judges Want You to Know (NBI, October, 2017).
- Co-Author (with Katelyn Holub), Television and Furniture Tip-Over Cases, 38 Verdict 2 (2017).
- Speaker, Television and Furniture Tip Over Claims (ITLA, May 2017).
- Speaker, Proving Pain, Suffering, and More in Personal Injury Litigation (NBI, Sept. 2016).
- Speaker, Advanced Issues in Personal Injury Litigation (NBI, December 2014).
- Speaker, Advanced Civil Litigation Skills in Indiana (NBI, Sept. 2015).
- Speaker, In the Trenches: Hearsay, Email, Business Records and Social Media (NBI, August, 2014).
- Speaker, Litigating Insurance Coverage Claims from Start to Finish (NBI, December, 2012).
- Speaker, Medicare Set-Asides in Personal Injury Litigation (NBI, October, 2011).
- Speaker, The Ambulance Intersection Case (ITLA, April 2010).

- Author, Preparing Dog Bite Cases, 28 Verdict 3 (2007).
- Author, The Rescue Doctrine, 30 Verdict 1 (2008).
- Co-author, Indiana Not-for-Profit Corporations: Standing to Maintain a Derivative Suit on Behalf of the Corporation, a Member's Suit to Enforce Membership Rights or a Citizen's Suit to Enforce Performance of Charitable Obligations, 25 Valparaiso University Law Review 249 (1991)
- Co-Author, Latent Heart Injury Following Vehicular Impact or Other Blunt Chest Trauma, 35 The Trial Lawyer's Guide 3 (Callaghan 1991).
- Author, The Contributory Negligence Defense as Applied Against Children in Indiana, 16 Valparaiso University Law Review 319-359 (1982).

Memberships:

Lake County and Indiana State Bar Associations; The Association of Trial Lawyers of America; Indiana Trial Lawyers Association; The National Trial Lawyers; The American Association for Justice; "The Multi-Million Dollar Advocates Forum – The Top Trial Lawyers in America." ™

Certifications: Board Certified by the National Board of Trial Advocacy as a Civil Trial Advocate (1996).

Katelyn Holub graduated *summa cum laude* from Valparaiso University's Christ College, the University's honors college. She majored in music and humanities and minored in physics. She received her J.D. from the Indiana University Robert H. McKinney School of Law.

While in law school, Ms. Holub was an editor for the *Indiana International and Comparative Law Review* and won the 2014 CALI Excellence for the Future Award by earning the highest grade in Payment Systems. Ms. Holub gained experience as a legal intern for the Indianapolis Museum of Art, doing work in copyright and trademark law, and for the Indiana State Department of Health, focusing on administrative law and health care law. Additionally, she interned in the corporate legal department of Indiana University Health, and later served as an intern to the Honorable Jane Magnus-Stinson, U.S. District Court Judge for the Southern District of Indiana.

Ms. Holub co-authored *Television and Furniture Tip-Over Cases*, 38 Verdict 2 (2017). She has volunteered in the Lake County Bar Association's Lawyers in the Classroom program by speaking at a local middle school for Law Day. She has also served as co-leader of her church's youth group and as a member of the praise band.

Ms. Holub is admitted to practice in the State of Indiana, the U.S. Federal District Courts for the Northern and Southern Districts of Indiana, the U.S. Court of Appeals for the Seventh Circuit, and is admitted to practice before the Supreme Court of the United States.

About the Firm

The Law Offices of David W. Holub is a personal injury law firm located in Merrillville, Indiana, focused on providing efficient and effective client-centered representation. Our mission is to provide top quality legal representation, which includes an uncompromising pursuit of our client's legal interests, while being accessible and attentive to our clients during times of personal challenge.

The firm concentrates in personal injury cases of all types, medical malpractice, and wrongful death litigation. We work tirelessly to serve each client aggressively and with empathy, to communicate regularly and clearly, and to obtain prompt and favorable results, while adhering to the highest standards of excellence and integrity. Our team considers it a high honor to be called upon to serve our clients whom we often come to regard as our friends.

The Law Offices of David W. Holub, P.C., strive to represent each client aggressively and to obtain prompt and favorable results. We not only aggressively pursue our client's best interests, but we remain accessible and attentive to our client's needs.

To learn more visit us at www.DavidHolubLaw.com or call us at (219) 736-9700.